COGNITIVE ATTACK SURFACE

The Mind's Vulnerabilities and How to Build Resilience Against Manipulation, Exploitation, and Delusion

KRINKEN ROHLEDER

Copyright © 2025 Krinken Rohleder
All Rights Reserved.

Contents

INTRODUCTION
The Most Vulnerable Frontier 1

PART I
UNDERSTANDING THE LANDSCAPE OF THE HUMAN MIND'S WEAKNESSES

CHAPTER 1
The Evolutionary Roots of Our Cognitive Vulnerabilities 5

CHAPTER 2
Delusion Drivers 29

CHAPTER 3
Mind Viruses and Social Contagion 45

CHAPTER 4
Digital Age Amplification of Cognitive Vulnerabilities 53

PART II
THE EXPLOITATION OF OUR MINDS' VULNERABILITIES

CHAPTER 5
The Art of Manipulation – From Persuasion to Coercion 59

CHAPTER 6
Self-Exploitation and Delusion 63

CHAPTER 7
Cybercrime and Perils of the Digital World 72

CHAPTER 8
Cults, Extremism, and the Erosion of Critical Thinking 86

CHAPTER 9
Misinformation, Disinformation, and the Information Warfare ... 97

CHAPTER 10
Politicians, Ideology, and the Weaponization of Identity 111

PART III
MITIGATING AGAINST COGNITIVE EXPLOITATION AND BUILDING RESILIENCY

CHAPTER 11
Individual Strategies for Cognitive Resilience   117

CHAPTER 12
Digital World Safety Guide   134

CHAPTER 13
Societal Solutions and Collective Resilience   144

CHAPTER 14
Ambassadors of Enlightenment 2.0   153

INTRODUCTION
The Most Vulnerable Frontier

Imagine a fortress, ancient and formidable, built over millennia to withstand the fiercest assaults. Its walls are thick, its defenses intricate. Now, imagine its most important, yet often overlooked, vulnerability, which is the minds of its inhabitants. Imagine, despite the impenetrable walls, the inhabitants are tricked into just opening the gates. In our increasingly interconnected world, the human mind has become the ultimate attack surface. We spend vast resources safeguarding our physical assets, digital networks, and financial data. Yet, the very core of our decision-making and beliefs, our minds remain remarkably exposed, often without us even realizing it.

This oversight is a growing threat in the information age, where ideas can spread globally at the speed of light. From the subtle nudges of advertising to the grand manipulations of political propaganda, from the insidious lures of online scams, to the nation-state level disinformation campaigns, our cognitive vulnerabilities are being exploited on an unprecedented scale. Bad actors are cheaply leveraging social media platforms to create anger and division. The stakes are high, ranging from individual regret and financial ruin to widespread societal fragmentation, erosion of trust, and even the collapse of rational discourse. These seemingly diverse suboptimal outcomes often share a common root: the exploitation of how we think.

This book serves as your guide to understanding the battlefield of the mind. We will explore the landscape of our cognitive vulnerabilities and the diverse and often sophisticated methods used to exploit them. More importantly, there are actionable strategies for individual and collective resilience. While this book is for anyone seeking to navigate the complexities of the modern information environment and how our minds work, it holds a special call for those who recognize the urgent need to support reason and truth. The paradox is that those who need this knowledge most are the least likely to seek it out. This book is for you, the reader who chose this book, and who I am asking to become an ambassador of enlightenment.

Cognitive Science and Cybersecurity

What is cognitive science, and how does it relate to cybersecurity? Cognitive Science is the interdisciplinary study of the mind and its processes, drawing insights from psychology, neuroscience, linguistics, philosophy, computer science, and anthropology to understand how we think, learn, remember, and perceive. It provides fundamental insights into the workings of our internal world. Conversely, cybersecurity is the practice of protecting systems, networks, and programs from digital attacks. It deals with concepts like vulnerability (a weakness in a system), exploit (a tool or technique that takes advantage of a vulnerability), and mitigation (strategies to reduce or eliminate risk from vulnerabilities and exploits).

By borrowing from cybersecurity's framework, we can better understand the threats to our minds. The urgent need for "cognitive security" has never been more pressing. In a world overflowing with information, the ability to think clearly, critically, and resiliently is not just a personal virtue but a societal necessity.

PART I
Understanding the Landscape of the Human Mind's Weaknesses

CHAPTER 1

The Evolutionary Roots of Our Cognitive Vulnerabilities

*"Man is a rational animal who always loses his temper
when he is called upon to act in accordance
with the dictates of reason."*
- Oscar Wilde

In the domain of cybersecurity, an "attack surface" refers to all the points or potential weaknesses where an unauthorized user can try to enter or extract data from an information system. For the human mind, our cognitive attack surface encompasses all our thinking. It encompasses how information enters our mind, is processed, and shapes our thinking, beliefs, and behaviors. When we speak of vulnerabilities in this context, we refer to inherent weaknesses or predispositions in our cognitive models that can be leveraged. A threat then becomes any potential exploit that 'utilizes' these weaknesses, intentional or not. This dynamic can be neatly summarized by the risk formula: **Risk = Vulnerability × Threat**

The greater our cognitive vulnerabilities, the higher the risk that a threat, whether a malicious actor, a misleading piece of information, or an unwitting error in judgment, will succeed in influencing us negatively.

A Story About a Woman Named Margaret

Margaret had always considered herself cautious. At 68, newly retired and living comfortably off her well-managed savings, she'd seen enough scams in the headlines to know the world was full of predators. But when the phone rang on a quiet Tuesday morning and a calm, professional voice claimed to be from her bank's fraud department, she didn't hesitate to listen.

The caller knew her name. Her bank. The last four digits of her account. He even referenced two recent transactions. There had been suspicious activity, he explained, and immediate action was needed to protect her funds. He spoke with measured urgency, not panic, but authority, and offered to help her transfer the money into a "protected" temporary account while the situation was investigated.

Margaret, still wary, asked for verification. The caller sent her a confirmation code from a number that matched her bank's contact info. With her fear rising and her trust deepening, she gave him what he asked for.

Within minutes, her entire retirement fund was gone.

What failed that day wasn't a firewall. It was Margaret's brain, which was doing exactly what it had evolved to do. The attacker didn't need malware. He used authority bias (the instinct to comply with perceived experts), loss aversion (our tendency to react more strongly to potential losses than gains), and the scarcity heuristic (the belief that immediate threats require immediate action). The initial framing is also important, which brings us to the primacy effect. The first information we receive about a person or situation disproportionately shapes our perception of what comes next. In Margaret's case, the scammer *led with credibility*: he had her name, account digits, and referenced real transactions. This early information framed the caller as legitimate, making all subsequent red flags easier to rationalize or ignore.

Once the brain has categorized someone as "safe" or "trustworthy," we unconsciously downgrade contradictory evidence. This makes it incredibly hard to reassess someone's trustworthiness once an initial impression is formed, especially under pressure.

He mimicked the patterns of trust: familiar names, insider details, the rhythm of urgency without chaos.

This wasn't a technical exploit; it was a cognitive exploit.

And that's the deeper danger. While most people believe they're rational actors, our decision-making is riddled with shortcuts such as heuristics, biases, and emotional triggers. These mechanisms are not merely inherent flaws; they are also, in many cases, efficient adaptations. But when placed in a digital environment designed to mimic authority, urgency, and credibility, these same adaptations become attack vectors. An attack vector in cybersecurity is the pathway or method that an attacker uses to gain unauthorized access to a network, system, or application, often to exploit vulnerabilities and carry out malicious activities like data theft or system compromise. A cognitive attack vector would be similar, where an attacker exploits a vulnerability of the mind, such as with the story of Margaret.

This is the cognitive attack surface in action. The vulnerability was a brain wired for trust in certain contexts. The threat was an actor skilled in deception and exploited the vulnerabilities. The resulting risk wasn't hypothetical. It was Margaret's life savings that evaporated in under five minutes. But why do we have these cognitive vulnerabilities?

The Evolutionary Roots of Our Cognitive Vulnerabilities

To truly grasp the reality of our cognitive attack surface, we first need to understand the remarkable machine that is the human brain and the deep history that shaped it. Cognitive science is this grand tapestry woven from various fields like psychology, neuroscience, linguistics, and even computer science, all assisting in comprehending the intricate processes of human thought. Human thought is shaped by specialized cognitive neural architectures. But we're lost without the proper context of where these highly specialized cognitive architectures came from.

This is where evolutionary psychology steps in. This field argues that our minds aren't blank slates; instead, they're the product of millions of years of natural selection. As researchers like David Buss have extensively documented, just as our bodies evolved to adapt to specific environments, our brains also evolved adaptive architectures and programming that we possess from birth. Our brains were optimized for survival and reproduction in our ancestral world. Understanding these deep-seated, inherited predispositions is needed to identify the very roots of our cognitive vulnerabilities.

Stubborn Orphaned Beliefs

Our cognitive structures can be thought of as miniature living systems. They have inherent defenses designed to maintain their own existence and consistency. Like all complex systems, they come with core attributes and boundary conditions. However, unlike perfectly logical machines, human cognitive systems don't just update instantly when they get new information. When we encounter something new, especially if it shifts our worldview, we don't perform a clean sweep of our mental landscape like an AI (Artificial Intelligence) would.

Instead, we often update selectively, leaving behind "orphaned beliefs" that no longer align with our broader understanding but still linger in the background. These orphaned, sticky beliefs are like outdated software running in the background of our minds. They persist because they once served a purpose and are part of our memory and emotional systems. Our brains are wired for efficiency, not perfect consistency. Updating a belief system takes real cognitive effort, and unless a belief is directly challenged, it might never be re-evaluated. Additionally, some orphaned beliefs may actually be grounded in survival, which would benefit us by changing more slowly.

Consider someone who has spent years studying emotional intelligence and healthy relationships. They understand the importance of setting boundaries and believe, on a rational level, that they deserve to be treated with respect. But when they find themselves in a relationship where their needs are ignored or their feelings dismissed, they still feel guilty for speaking up. They make excuses for the other person's behavior and question whether they are overreacting.

This reaction doesn't come from their current understanding. It comes from an older belief, likely formed in childhood, that love must be earned or that being good means avoiding conflict. Even though their conscious beliefs have evolved, that outdated emotional response remains active beneath the surface. The belief no longer fits, but it continues to influence behavior.

However, not all orphaned beliefs are dysfunctional. Sometimes, the belief that no longer fits with a new worldview might still be valid or even wise. Imagine someone raised in a home where financial caution was a core value. They were taught to save diligently, avoid debt, and prepare for uncertainty. Later in life, they adopt a more entrepreneurial mindset influenced by risk-taking, aggressive investing, and optimistic messaging about abundance.

The old belief about caution may now feel outdated or limiting, especially in circles that celebrate bold financial risk. But when the economy takes a downturn or a speculative investment collapses, that quiet, persistent caution can become a source of stability and resilience. What seemed like an unnecessary fear might turn out to be a hard-earned form of wisdom.

This is why orphaned beliefs should not be discarded blindly. Just because a belief no longer aligns with our current identity does not mean it is wrong. Each belief, whether inherited, outdated, or forgotten, deserves to be examined on its own terms, separate from the worldview that replaced it. Our brain evolution, development, and structure support this sort of multimodality of slowly changing emotional anchors and quickly adapting thinking. We, in the context of evolution, have different parts of our brain that are from different eras.

The brain can be understood in terms of its evolutionary development, with the oldest parts forming the core and the newest parts representing complex adaptations. The brain stem, the most ancient and primitive part of the brain, governs essential, involuntary functions for survival like breathing, heart rate, and consciousness. Think of it as the "reptilian brain" that all vertebrates share, ensuring the basic machinery of life is running. Above that sits the midbrain, which evolved to process sensory information and control motor movements. It acts as a relay center, coordinating responses to visual and auditory stimuli and linking the primitive brain stem with the more advanced forebrain. The cortex, especially the neocortex, is the newest and largest part of the human brain. It's responsible for higher-level functions like language, abstract thought, problem-solving, and conscious awareness. The dramatic expansion and folding of the cortex in humans enabled complex social behaviors, tool use, and the development of culture, distinguishing us from other species.

Cognitive Dissonance and Internal Inconsistency

This phenomenon of orphaned beliefs is deeply connected to cognitive dissonance, the psychological discomfort we feel when we hold two or more conflicting beliefs, values, or attitudes, especially when our behavior contradicts one of them. This internal tension motivates us to reduce the inconsistency, often by changing our beliefs, justifying our behavior, or minimizing the importance of the conflict. For instance, someone who values health but smokes might rationalize their habit by downplaying the risks or convincing themselves that quitting is too stressful. Cognitive dissonance reveals our very human drive for internal consistency and how we mentally navigate contradictions in our thoughts and actions.

Fragmentation of beliefs leads to inconsistencies that our minds often try to compartmentalize rather than resolve. This fragmentation can create internal tension or blind spots within our thinking. In cybersecurity terms, it's like patching the main system but leaving legacy vulnerabilities unaddressed, which is an attacker's dream. In personal development, it means we might act in ways that contradict our stated values or goals without ever realizing why.

What is the 'Mismatch Hypothesis' in Evolutionary Psychology?

Our brains, honed by the pressures of ancient environments, were selected for rapid decision-making in a world of immediate threats and limited information. This ancient neural architecture, incredibly effective for dodging predators or finding food, is often spectacularly ill-equipped for the complexities, abstractions, and overwhelming amount of information that exists in the modern age. We are living in an era for which our brains were simply not designed. Our stone-aged brain is running outdated software and is trying to solve 21st-century problems. This mismatch creates a host of modern dysfunctions.

What are some of these modern dysfunctions from our stone-aged brain?

- **Information Overload (Cognitive Fatigue)**
  Our ancestors had to process only small, relevant chunks of information, such as tracking animal movements, weather shifts, or social cues within a tribe. Today, we're bombarded with notifications, headlines, emails, ads, and decisions that are far more stimuli than our brains evolved to handle. The result? Mental exhaustion, decision fatigue, and anxiety.

- **Social Comparison (Chronic Insecurity)**
In small tribal groups, social comparison helped us gauge our standing and improve our chances of survival. Now, we scroll past curated lives of thousands online, triggering feelings of inadequacy, envy, and low self-worth despite knowing it's a highlight reel.

- **Immediate Rewards (Addiction and Procrastination)**
Our dopamine systems evolved to reward us for actions like finding sweet fruit or mating, which are things that had clear survival value. Today, the same systems are hijacked by apps, junk food, porn, and streaming services, creating addictive loops and undermining long-term goals.

- **Tribal Thinking (Polarization and Echo Chambers)**
The brain naturally categorizes people into "us" vs. "them" to enhance group cohesion. In the modern world, this fuels political polarization, racism, and online echo chambers, which are not adaptive in a globally interconnected society.

- **Negativity Bias (Chronic Fear and Anxiety)**
Being hyper-alert to threats helped avoid predators or rival attacks. Now, with 24/7 news cycles feeding us disasters, crises, and outrage, our brains remain in a near-constant fight-or-flight mode that is leading to elevated stress levels and health consequences. We did not evolve in an environment where we knew every bad thing that was happening in the entire world.

- **Pattern Recognition (Conspiracy Thinking)**
Spotting patterns, like footprints or rustling in the bushes, once meant survival. But now, the same instinct can lead us to false correlations, magical thinking, and conspiracies, especially when paired with uncertainty or fear.

- **Short-Term Thinking (Climate Inaction and Poor Planning)**
  Evolution rewarded immediate gratification and survival over long-term planning. That's a problem in a world where solving major issues (like climate change or retirement savings) requires thinking decades ahead.

Tribalism

Social psychologists like Henri Tajfel and John Turner, through their work on social identity theory, have extensively documented how these deep evolutionary roots manifest today as powerful, often subconscious, predispositions towards group identification and conformity, a formidable vulnerability in a globalized, diverse society.

Human tribalism is indeed deeply embedded in our evolutionary history. Much of what we see in people's behavior today is a testament to this. For millions of years, early humans lived in small, tightly bonded groups where survival hinged on loyalty and group cohesion. According to psychologist Jessica Koehler, our ancestors' survival often depended on how well they aligned with the group's shared beliefs and behaviors. Those who failed to conform either by rejecting group norms or acting independently often faced banishment or even death, effectively removing them from the gene pool. This created powerful evolutionary pressure for conformity and strong in-group bias.

Neuroscientist Justin James Kennedy builds on this idea, explaining that the structure of the human brain itself was shaped to favor tribal loyalty. He emphasizes that conformity wasn't just a cultural habit; it became biologically reinforced. As the human brain evolved, particularly in size and complexity, it allowed for more sophisticated social behaviors but also cemented mechanisms that prioritize group identity and allegiance.

This trend is further supported by the Smithsonian Institution's Human Origins Program, which notes that as early humans encountered new environmental and social challenges, their brains tripled in size. This growth enabled more complex thinking and social interaction, which in turn made tribal coordination more sophisticated and deeply rooted in our cognitive architecture.

Kennedy also highlights the role of neuroplasticity, which is the brain's ability to change in response to experience. Our brains are not only shaped by evolution but also by the cultures and environments we live in. Cultural studies in neuroscience show that individuals from different cultural backgrounds exhibit distinct patterns of brain activation during social interactions, reinforcing the idea that our tribal tendencies are both biologically hardwired and culturally reinforced.

The Power of Identity - Party Over Policy

The inherent human inclination towards tribalism, while deeply rooted in our evolutionary past, finds stark and powerful expression in the modern world. Tribal identity, once triggered, can override rational thought, even when it comes to concrete policy issues.

Research in social psychology vividly illustrates this "party over policy" effect. A seminal study by Geoffrey L. Cohen (2003), among others, demonstrated how individuals' agreement with a particular policy proposal can hinge almost entirely on which political party is perceived to endorse it, rather than on the policy's actual content or its alignment with their personal beliefs.

In such experiments, participants are presented with a policy whose details are crafted to potentially appeal to various ideological viewpoints or are kept intentionally neutral. The manipulation came when participants were informed that either their own political party or an opposing party supported the policy. The findings were remarkable. Individuals are significantly more likely to endorse and favor a policy when they believe it is championed by their own political group. Conversely, the very same policy often faces strong disapproval when supported by an opposing party. This occurs even when the policy's details might, upon objective review, contradict the individual's stated ideology, or when it is identical to a policy they previously rejected under a different partisan label. Participants would remarkably shift their views, either withdrawing support upon learning a policy belonged to an opposing party, or endorsing it when attributed to their own, regardless of initial disposition.

This phenomenon underscores the profound influence of partisan motivated reasoning, where the desire to maintain group allegiance and uphold one's tribal identity overshadows a dispassionate evaluation of facts or merits. We will learn about motivated reasoning and strategic optimizers later. Basically, the party label acts as a powerful cognitive shortcut, dictating judgment and reinforcing the in-group bias that is fundamental to our tribal wiring. This dynamic reveals a formidable challenge in a globalized, diverse society, where rational discourse on complex issues can be derailed by deeply ingrained loyalties to political, social, or cultural tribes.

Together, these findings reveal that our brains are naturally inclined toward tribalism. This innate bias is further amplified by modern forces like political identity, emotional rhetoric, and cognitive framing.

Identifying a Tribalism Mindset

You can often identify a tribal mindset when someone speaks in broad generalities and stereotypes rather than considering individuals or nuance. They may frame issues in stark "us versus them" terms, portraying their own side as righteous and the other as dangerous, ignorant, or corrupt. Instead of weighing evidence or acknowledging complexity, their language emphasizes loyalty, group identity, and division, making disagreement feel like betrayal rather than a difference of perspective.

Examples of phrases that often signal a tribal mindset:
- *"People like them are all the same."*
- *"Our side actually cares about the truth, unlike theirs."*
- *"You can't trust anyone from that group."*
- *"We're the real [patriots/believers/workers], they're just out to destroy everything."*
- *"If you're not with us, you're against us."*
- *"That's exactly what people like you would say."*

These kinds of statements reduce individuals to categories, ignore nuance, and reinforce a partisan, "in-group versus out-group" worldview.

Consider the following language: *The Greens always put trees before people.* Notice the generality and how the language gives agency to a group as though it were an individual. The greens, that is all greens, anyone who identifies as them or believes as they do, always, that is without exception, put trees before people, which obviously means they (all of them) have their priorities wrong. As bad as this overgeneralized thinking is, consider how it might trigger a bad tribalistic response. Consider the following language: *The Builders always want to tear down nature, even when it will lead to all of our destruction.* So, someone who might identify as a Green might get triggered and generalize and give agency to Builders who, similarly, are always thinking and doing the same thing, without nuance or complexity of thought. In a way, this type of tribal back and forth does reduce the thinking to very basic and binary outputs that do, in fact, lack nuance. It is a sort of self-fulfilling prophecy. These two imaginary people would be talking past each other and dehumanizing each other.

Anonymity, Cars, Social Media, and Tribalism

Humans often behave differently when they are anonymous compared to when they are face-to-face, a phenomenon supported by research in social psychology. This shift in behavior is primarily due to the deindividuation effect, a concept first introduced by psychologist Leon Festinger. Deindividuation is a state where individuals lose their sense of personal identity and responsibility when in a group or when their actions are not attributable to them personally. The lack of accountability and fear of social repercussions that are present in face-to-face interactions are significantly reduced, leading people to act in ways they wouldn't normally. A notable study by psychologist Philip Zimbardo demonstrated this effect in his Stanford Prison Experiment, where participants assigned to the guard role engaged in increasingly aggressive behavior due to their anonymity and perceived power within the group. Face-to-face interaction does not just enforce accountability; it triggers a different brain state altogether and promotes bonding.

Modern car culture and social media have greatly amplified opportunities for anonymous interaction, thereby increasing the prevalence of deindividuation. Driving, for instance, provides a physical and psychological barrier. The anonymity of being in a vehicle, combined with a lack of personal connection with other drivers, can lead to aggressive behaviors like road rage. Similarly, social media platforms create a sense of detachment. Users can hide behind avatars or pseudonyms, which diminishes their sense of personal accountability. This anonymity often fuels online bullying, harassment, and the spread of misinformation, as individuals feel emboldened to post things they wouldn't dare say in person.

The impact of this increased anonymity on the modern world is profound. It has contributed to a more polarized and often hostile online environment, where civil discourse is replaced by malicious attacks. The erosion of face-to-face interactions in favor of digital communication also risks weakening social cohesion and empathy. Human bonding and moral development require face-to-face interactions with all the necessary cues to initiate healthy brain states. As people become more accustomed to anonymous or impersonal interactions, they may lose the skills needed for effective in-person communication and conflict resolution. This can lead to a society that is more isolated, less tolerant, and more prone to conflict, as the safeguards of social norms and personal accountability are increasingly absent.

This anonymity and deindividuation also feed into tribalism and the dehumanization of others. When people interact anonymously, it becomes easier to view others not as individuals but as faceless members of an out-group. This psychological distancing makes it simpler to justify hostility and aggression toward those with different views. For example, on social media platforms, political opponents or members of a different community are often reduced to stereotypes, making it easier to dismiss their perspectives and engage in hateful rhetoric. This erodes the empathy and nuanced understanding needed for civil discourse, leading to a more polarized and hostile social environment where a sense of shared humanity is lost.

Cognitive Biases

A significant consequence of this evolutionary heritage is our reliance on heuristics and biases, which are cognitive shortcuts. To cope with the sheer volume of information and the need for quick decisions, our brains developed mental shortcuts, heuristics, which are generally efficient but can lead to predictable errors or biases, especially in unfamiliar or complex situations. Pioneering research by psychologists Daniel Kahneman and Amos Tversky laid the groundwork for much of our understanding of these cognitive shortcuts.

Some examples of cognitive bias

- **Availability Heuristic:** We overestimate the likelihood of events based on how easily examples come to mind (for example, fearing plane crashes

more than car accidents because they are more vividly reported in news reports).
- **Confirmation Bias:** We seek out, interpret, and remember information in a way that confirms our existing beliefs, while ignoring contradictory evidence. This bias has been robustly demonstrated across various studies.
- **Anchoring Effect:** Our judgments are unduly influenced by the first piece of information we encounter, even if it is irrelevant. This effect is a cornerstone of negotiation and pricing strategies.
- **Framing Effect:** Our decisions are influenced by how information is presented, even if the underlying facts are the same. Kahneman and Tversky's Prospect Theory highlights how different frames can lead to different risk appetites.
- **Dunning-Kruger Effect:** Studies by psychologists David Dunning and Justin Kruger revealed that individuals with low ability in a task overestimate their own ability, while high-ability individuals often underestimate theirs.
- **Bandwagon Effect:** We adopt beliefs or behaviors because many other people do, regardless of the underlying evidence. This is a classic finding in social psychology, akin to Solomon Asch's work on conformity.
- **Halo Effect:** Our overall impression of a person, company, or product influences our feelings and thoughts about their character or qualities (for example, if someone is attractive, we assume they are also kind). Edward Thorndike first coined this term.

In contrast to cognitive shortcuts for mental conservation, naturally selected biases likely offered survival advantages in ancestral environments. Tribalism, for instance, fostered cohesion. The Endowment Effect, documented by Kahneman, Knetsch, and Thaler, describes the tendency to overvalue things we own. The Endowment Effect reflects an evolutionarily selected cognitive bias, where in environments of scarcity, individuals disproportionately valued and defended resources they already possessed. This increased their chances of survival and reproduction through self-serving promotion of their owned resources. Other biases might have been neutral, neither significantly hindering nor aiding survival, and thus simply persisted.

Dual Processing Theory

One useful insight into our cognitive architecture comes from Daniel Kahneman's Dual Processing Theory (System 1 & System 2), extensively detailed in his book *Thinking, Fast and Slow*.

- **System 1:** This is our fast, unconscious, automatic, intuitive, and emotional mode of thinking. It is the system that allows us to recognize a face, react to a sudden noise, or solve a simple math problem without conscious effort. It is efficient but prone to biases.
- **System 2:** This is our slow, conscious, methodical, logical, and rational mode of thinking. It is engaged when we solve complex problems, deliberate over important decisions, or learn a new skill. It requires effort and attention.

Interestingly, while System 2 often *thinks* it is in charge, System 1 frequently "manipulates and undermines" it. System 1 generates impressions, intuitions, intentions, and feelings, and if System 2 is busy, distracted, or simply lazy, it will often uncritically endorse these suggestions. This highlights System 1's ultimate, pervasive control in many situations, making it a prime target for cognitive exploitation.

This division can be illustrated as a tension between the need for speed vs. the need for accuracy. Our evolutionary drive for rapid decision-making in a dangerous world meant that speed often trumped meticulous accuracy. In modern scenarios, particularly those designed to induce urgency, this can lead to significant errors. Think about how cybersecurity criminals use phishing schemes: they create a sense of immediate threat or opportunity to bypass System 2's critical analysis and trigger System 1's fast, often fear-driven, response.

"Urgent Payroll Update" Phishing Email

Imagine you're at work, sorting through a backlog of emails. Suddenly, you see this subject line:

"Action Required: Your Paycheck Will Be Delayed – Update Info Now!"

When you click, the email looks official and has the same logo as your company's payroll provider, the same tone, and even a footer with HR contact info.

It says:

"Due to a recent security update, we need you to confirm your direct deposit information to avoid payroll processing delays. Failure to act within the next 2 hours will result in a delay to your next paycheck. Click here to verify."

In that moment, your **System 1** fast, automatic, emotionally reactive brain jumps into action. You feel a spike of anxiety: *"I can't afford a missed paycheck!"*
You click the link and fill in your details without slowing down to question anything.

What just happened?

- **System 1** took over: Fear + urgency = rapid action.
- **System 2**—your slow, logical, skeptical mind—never got a chance to step in and ask, *"Wait, does HR normally contact me this way?"*

This is why phishing works since it hijacks evolved survival instincts, responding to threats fast, avoiding loss, trusting authority signals, all to short-circuit deliberate thinking.

Memory

Another vulnerability lies in the nature of our memory. Extensive research by cognitive psychologists, notably Elizabeth Loftus, has demonstrated that our memory has not evolved for perfect accuracy or as some pristine recording of reality. Instead, it is more about relationships, associations, and creating a coherent narrative. The brain can, and frequently does, distort, manipulate, or downright invent a memory to fulfill a current need, often serving our survival and reproductive strategies. This means our recollections are not always reliable archives but rather dynamic constructions, susceptible to influence and even the implantation of false memories.

Framing as the Brain's Apps

The brain's tendency to organize information into meaningful structures is evident in cognitive framing. Framing is like an app that runs in the brain. Just as a smartphone app organizes a particular set of functions, specific cues and contexts can trigger mental "frames" that significantly influence how we perceive and interpret information. For example, presenting a medical procedure as having a "90% survival rate" evokes a different frame and emotional response than presenting it as having a "10% mortality rate," even though the statistics are identical. Our dual processing systems interact with framing; a System 1 response can quickly activate a particular frame, which then biases subsequent System 2 processing.

The Pattern Seeking Brain

We see patterns everywhere! Have you ever sat and looked up at the clouds with a friend and shared what images you see in their shapes? The phenomenon of Pareidolia, the tendency to perceive patterns or significance in random or meaningless data (like seeing faces in clouds or religious figures on toast), is a clear example of a cognitive vulnerability rooted in our brains' efficient pattern recognition. Closely related is apophenia, which is the spontaneous perception of connections and meaningfulness in unrelated phenomena. Why would evolution select this? Simply put, in an ancestral environment, falsely detecting a pattern, for example, a predator hiding in the tall grass, was less costly than failing to detect a real one. The advantage of survival from pattern recognition in overdrive, with occasional false positives, has built this tendency into the architecture of our brain. One common type of pattern recognition bias is our tendency to see agency everywhere.

Agency Errors

We are born with a strong tendency towards making agency errors, which is our tendency to anthropomorphize things and attribute intentionality. A shadow in the night could just be a shadow, but our brains are wired to consider the possibility of a predator. There is a natural selection asymmetry at play: being overly paranoid about agency in ambiguous situations was often advantageous. This means we are predisposed to see agents and intentions where none exist, making us susceptible to narratives that attribute grand designs to random events or even supernatural forces.

Abstraction Errors

Humans also frequently fall victim to Abstraction Errors, arguing, thinking, or comparing things at the wrong level of abstraction. Evolution favored abstraction and generalization as efficient ways to categorize and predict.

Think about how easily we can go into any kitchen and cook, despite all the utensils being of different styles and ingredients being stored in different drawers. Our brains are adept at forming cognitive categories, often at a "mid-level" of processing, like in the Gavagai problem. The *Gavagai problem* is a philosophical thought experiment introduced by W.V.O. Quine to illustrate the deep ambiguity inherent in language and translation. Imagine an anthropologist observing a foreign culture. A native points to a rabbit and exclaims, "Gavagai!" It seems straightforward to assume that "gavagai" means "rabbit." However, as Quine points out, there is no definitive way to determine this. The word could just as easily mean "the color brown," "running," "fuzzy creature," or even "dinner." All of these interpretations are logically consistent with the observation. This leads to Quine's thesis of the indeterminacy of translation: there is no objective fact that determines exactly what individual words refer to, and multiple, equally valid interpretations can coexist. The Gavagai problem reveals, from a pure computational viewpoint, how meaning is not fixed but arises from a web of beliefs, context, and assumptions. It challenges the idea that words have simple, one-to-one correspondences with objects in the world and has broad implications for philosophy, linguistics, cognitive science, and artificial intelligence, especially in understanding how language is grounded in experience. In the context of evolutionary psychology, mid-level processing bias and grammatical structures are innate. This is why a child can learn with several orders of magnitude less information than an AI system. The brain has specifically evolved architectures that determine innate context. It is not just our individual experience that determines our interpretations, but the experience of our ancestors is built into our DNA.

Barnum Effect: An Abstraction Error

Cognitive efficiency through abstraction can lead to pitfalls like the Barnum Effect, also known as the Forer effect, where vague, general statements are perceived as highly accurate and personal by a wide audience. Consider the story of the Oracle of Willow Creek.

The Oracle of Willow Creek

Elara, a self-proclaimed psychic, set up her tent at the annual Willow Creek Fair, promising personalized readings. Her secret wasn't supernatural ability, but a keen understanding of human psychology, specifically cognitive efficiency and its pitfalls.

A young man named Liam approached, skepticism written on his face. Elara gazed into her crystal ball. "I sense," she began, her voice low and resonant, "a strong desire for security, but also a hidden yearning for adventure. You've experienced both successes and disappointments, and sometimes you question if you're truly on the right path."

Liam's eyes widened. "That's... incredibly accurate!" he exclaimed, a blush rising on his cheeks. He *did* want financial security, but secretly dreamt of backpacking through South America. He *had* recently aced an exam but also messed up a job interview. Every word resonated.

Next was an older woman, Mrs. Gable, a pillar of the community. Elara, without missing a beat, offered a similar reading. "You have a deep sense of responsibility to others," she intoned, "and sometimes you put their needs before your own. You've overcome significant challenges in your life, and while you project strength, there are moments of self-doubt."

Mrs. Gable nodded tearfully. "It's true! How did you know?" She thought of her years volunteering, her sacrifices for her family, and the quiet anxieties she kept hidden.

Elara smiled inwardly. She wasn't seeing their pasts or futures. She was simply delivering vague, general statements. These statements were so broad that they could apply to almost anyone. Liam's brain, seeking meaning and efficiency, unconsciously abstracted these generalities, filling in the gaps with his own specific experiences. Mrs. Gable's mind performed the same trick, making the fuzzy pronouncements feel highly accurate and personal. They didn't see Elara's clever use of cognitive efficiency through abstraction; they were experiencing the classic Barnum Effect. And Elara, the "Oracle," was doing a roaring trade.

Overgeneralization and stereotyping, while sometimes useful cognitive shortcuts for quickly categorizing the world, are potent sources of misleading thinking. How does tribalism leverage these? By painting entire "out-groups" with broad, often negative, strokes, and attributing agency to abstract "groups" rather than individuals, we can dehumanize anyone belonging to these groups. This tendency to speak in generalizations about groups, as if "groups" themselves possess agency, is basically anthropomorphizing a cognitive construct. Only individuals have agency, not categories or groups. The abstraction error and agency error allowed tribal groups to commit atrocities when resources were scarce. We bypassed our empathy by creating an abstract, dehumanized villain.

The outgroup homogeneity effect is the tendency to view members of an outgroup (people outside your own group) as more similar to each other, in beliefs, behaviors, or traits, than they actually are, while seeing members of your ingroup (your own group) as diverse and nuanced. This means our own group seems more human to us. Studies in social identity and prejudice suggest we are indeed optimized for overgeneralization and stereotyping due to our tribal evolution.

Strategic Optimizers

Our brain has strategic algorithms that we will call optimizers. These intelligent strategic optimizers manipulate our thinking and reasoning to solve problems. Drawing on insights from behavioral economics and social psychology, including work by researchers like Ziva Kunda and Dan Kahan on motivated reasoning, we understand that these are not conscious decisions but deeply ingrained, strategic algorithms within the brain that constantly "solve" for a variety of needs and drives. While we often perceive ourselves as driven purely by the pursuit of truth, our brains are in fact continuously optimizing for a multitude of goals, many of which are rooted in evolved imperatives. This means that our reasoning is rarely, if ever, a neutral, objective process. Instead, it is almost always "motivated," shaped by these underlying optimizers, which often have objectives far removed from simply uncovering factual reality. While "discovery" or "truth" optimizers certainly exist and lead us to genuinely seek objective reality, they are frequently shut down by other types of optimizers.

Here are some strategic optimizers driving motivated reasoning:

- **Ego Optimizers:** Reasoning designed to protect our self-image, save face, or maintain social status. This often means twisting facts or avoiding information that might diminish our standing.
- **Tribal Identity Optimizers:** Reasoning to defend beliefs dictated by our group or political identity, prioritizing group cohesion and loyalty over individual accuracy. We defend our "tribe's" beliefs even if they lack sound evidence.
- **Belief Optimizers:** Reasoning to protect existing beliefs, even in the face of contradictory evidence, because challenging them can be cognitively uncomfortable and require significant mental effort.
- **Worldview Optimizers:** Reasoning to maintain the consistency of our overarching worldview, resisting anything that might destabilize the carefully constructed narrative through which we understand the world.
- **Fear Optimizers:** Reasoning driven by fear, leading to irrational decisions or the acceptance of comforting falsehoods that alleviate anxiety, even if they are untrue.

- **Prejudice Optimizers:** Reasoning influenced by existing biases and animosity towards certain groups, leading to interpretations of information that confirm pre-existing negative stereotypes.
- **Self-Interest Optimizers:** Reasoning aimed at maintaining money, power, or personal gain associated with a particular belief or course of action, even if it requires intellectual dishonesty.

These "optimizers" are not always conscious choices; they are often subconscious drives that shape our interpretation of information, leading to what is broadly known as motivated reasoning. These types of reasoning are not about discovering the truth, but rather about arriving at a solution that serves one of these underlying motivations.

CHAPTER 2

Delusion Drivers

"It is hard to free fools from the chains they revere."
– Voltaire

Our minds are not just processors of raw data; they are relentless meaning-makers. We are not merely observers of reality but active constructors of it. We have drivers that initiate optimization for a coherent and self-interested understanding of the world. This can also be a profound source of vulnerability, leading us down paths of deeply held, yet factually unfounded, beliefs. This is the realm of delusion.

The Storytelling Brain

Our meaning-making tendency yields what neuroscientists and psychologists refer to as "the storytelling brain". Michael Gazzaniga's groundbreaking split-brain research, for instance, revealed the remarkable "interpreter" module, primarily located in the left hemisphere. When Gazzaniga's patients, whose brain hemispheres were surgically separated, performed actions directed by the right hemisphere (which controls the left side of the body and has limited linguistic ability), their left hemisphere would instantly concoct plausible, yet entirely fabricated, explanations for those actions. For example, if the right hemisphere was prompted to make the left-hand point to a picture, the left hemisphere would invent a rational narrative for why the patient chose that picture, even though it had no direct knowledge of the original command.

This "interpreter" isn't unique to split-brain patients; it's constantly at work in all of us. Our brains dislike a vacuum of meaning. When faced with incomplete information, ambiguous events, or even contradictory experiences, this innate storyteller steps in, weaving narratives to fill gaps, impose order, and create a sense of understanding. This process is largely automatic and unconscious. We crave causality and coherence, and if a clear, factual explanation isn't readily available, our brains will simply invent one that fits our existing framework, often without our conscious awareness. This means that a significant portion of what we believe to be true might be a compelling story our brain has told itself, rather than a direct reflection of reality.

How Our Own Storytelling Narratives Can Misconstrue Reality

Consider Sarah, a marketing executive who prides herself on her rational decision-making. One Tuesday, she arrives at work feeling unusually irritable. Throughout the morning, minor annoyances such as a slow elevator, a lukewarm coffee, and a colleague's offhand comment all seem to disproportionately grate on her nerves. By lunchtime, she's convinced her colleague, Mark, is deliberately undermining her. She recalls several instances from the past week where Mark seemed to interrupt her in meetings or disagree with her proposals, and suddenly, these scattered events coalesce into a clear narrative: Mark is trying to sabotage her career.

What Sarah doesn't consciously realize is that her irritability that morning stemmed from a restless night's sleep, brought on by a late-night work session. Her brain, seeking an explanation for her internal state, didn't have immediate access to the true cause (lack of sleep). Instead, her "interpreter" began scanning her environment for a plausible external reason for her discomfort. Mark's past interactions, though likely innocuous at the time, were readily available data points. The brain then wove these into a coherent, albeit entirely fabricated, story of Mark's supposed malice. Sarah's brain craved a reason for her feeling, and it found one that fit neatly into an easily digestible narrative, even if it wasn't the objective truth. She genuinely believes Mark is out to get her, not because of his actions, but because her own brain has constructed a compelling story to explain her internal discomfort.

Narratives and why a 'Worldview' is a Matrix of Delusion

The individual narratives spun by our storytelling brains coalesce into larger, more complex structures: our "Worldview". A worldview is essentially our personal operating system, a comprehensive framework of beliefs, values, and assumptions through which we interpret everything. It shapes our perceptions, influences our judgments, and dictates how we respond to new information. Psychologists often describe worldviews as resistant to change because they provide a sense of stability and meaning. When new information challenges a core aspect of our worldview, it can trigger significant psychological discomfort.

Instead of dismantling the entire framework, our minds often engage in mental gymnastics to preserve it. We may selectively attend to information that confirms our existing view, dismiss contradictory evidence as unreliable, or reinterpret conflicting data to fit our narrative. This moves us away from seeing the world as it really is. This process is amplified by social pressure from our in-group (tribalism). Our desire to belong to a group and conform to its norms can exert immense pressure to adopt and maintain a shared worldview, even if it contains inaccuracies. Deviating from the group's narrative risks social ostracism, a powerful disincentive for our evolutionarily wired social brains.

The Nature of Belief

How do these powerful beliefs form and solidify? Beliefs are not merely intellectual propositions; they are deeply intertwined with our emotions, experiences, and social connections. Research by scholars like Jonathan Haidt on moral psychology suggests that beliefs often form instinctively, based on intuition and emotion, with reason then serving as an *ex post facto* justification. Beliefs solidify through:

- **Repetition:** The more often we hear something, the more familiar and, consequently, more believable it becomes (the "illusory truth effect").
- **Emotional Attachment:** Beliefs tied to strong emotions, positive or negative, are far more resistant to change.
- **Social Reinforcement:** When our beliefs are validated by our social group, they gain immense strength and become part of our shared reality.

Once formed, beliefs can become integral to our very identity. To challenge a deeply held belief can feel like an attack on who we are, activating our ego and tribal identity optimizers, making us even more resistant to contradictory evidence.

Tribalism - The Powerful Drive to Belong

Building on the foundation laid in Chapter 1, tribalism is a profound and ancient force that continues to shape our cognition and behavior. The "us vs. them" mentality is not merely a social construct; it is a deeply embedded neurological predisposition. As social identity theory, proposed by Henri Tajfel and John Turner, illustrates, people derive a significant part of their self-concept from the groups they belong to. We categorize ourselves and others, and we naturally favor our in-group while often devaluing or stereotyping the out-group. This leads to in-group/out-group biases, where we perceive our own group members as more diverse and positive, while viewing out-group members as more homogenous and potentially negative.

Consider the metaphor of a "tribalism app" running in your brain. When activated, perhaps by a thought-terminating cliche, a heated online debate, or even a news headline framed in terms of group conflict, this "app" fundamentally changes our brain state and cognitive framing. It can suppress individual critical thinking, prioritize group loyalty, and make us more receptive to information that supports our tribe, even if that information is flawed. The feeling of belonging, being part of a collective identity, is so powerful that it can override rational thought and even personal moral convictions. The dopamine hit from tribal validation reinforces this behavior, making us seek out more of it.

Identity and Ideology

Our sense of self, our identity, is profoundly intertwined with our beliefs and group affiliations. We are not just individuals; we are members of families, communities, nations, and ideological camps. These affiliations provide us with meaning, purpose, and a sense of belonging.

An ideology is more than just a belief system; it is a comprehensive framework that offers a simplified version of reality with rules that are easy for cognitive processing. Think of it as an "information compression of reality." Our storytelling brains, eager to make sense of the complex world, readily fill in any inconsistencies with stories that fit the ideological narrative. For example, a complex economic issue might be reduced to a simple good-versus-evil narrative, blaming an "out-group" rather than acknowledging nuanced systemic factors.

An ideology can function as a "virtual cognitive cult." While perhaps not as overtly coercive as a traditional cult, it leverages some of the same psychological mechanisms: a clear narrative, a defined in-group and out-group, shared values, and a strong sense of identity derived from adherence to the system. It is important to note that ideologies are cognitive constructs that are mostly blunt tools for helping us understand reality. They should not be used to dictate how we live our lives as though they are the absolute truth. They serve powerful drivers for identity, offering quick answers, tribal bonding, and a sense of certainty in an uncertain world.

Cognitive Dissonance

As we read earlier, the psychological discomfort arising from holding conflicting beliefs or from beliefs conflicting with actions is known as cognitive dissonance, a theory first proposed by Leon Festinger in 1957. This discomfort drives us to reduce the inconsistency.

For instance, a person who strongly believes in environmental protection but frequently drives a large, gas-guzzling SUV might experience cognitive dissonance. To resolve this, they might justify their behavior by arguing they *need* a large vehicle for their family rather than changing their driving habits or vehicle. Cognitive dissonance highlights our brain's strong drive for internal consistency, even if it requires distorting reality.

Sticky Beliefs, Inconsistency, and Compartmentalization

As discussed in Chapter 1, sticky beliefs are those that resist updating, even when new information should logically alter them. Cognitive dissonance is a primary reason for their persistence. The brain deals with this dissonance not always by direct resolution, but often through selective belief retention, ignoring contradictions, and compartmentalization. Compartmentalization is the psychological defense mechanism of keeping conflicting ideas, values, or emotions separate in our minds, thereby avoiding the cognitive dissonance they would otherwise cause. A person might hold strong, contradictory political views but keep them in separate "mental boxes" to avoid confronting the inconsistency. This allows the brain to maintain a semblance of consistency within specific contexts, even if the overall worldview is fragmented.

Defense Mechanisms and Logical Fallacies

When our core beliefs, ego, tribal identity, or worldview are threatened, our minds deploy a range of defense mechanisms. A defense mechanism is a type of evolved strategic optimizer. These are often unconscious strategies that prioritize self-preservation and group cohesion over objective truth. These defenses often manifest as the strategic use of logical fallacies.

Unlike cognitive biases, which are often unconscious shortcuts our brains take, logical fallacies can be deployed intentionally (though often still subconsciously) as rhetorical strategies to defend a position, deflect criticism, or manipulate an argument. They are systematic, and sometimes intentional, errors in reasoning.

Top Logical Fallacies

- **Ad Hominem Attack:** Attacking the person making the argument rather than the argument itself ("You can't trust anything he says; he's a terrible person!"). This defends ego or tribal identity by discrediting the source.
- **Straw Man Fallacy:** Misrepresenting an opponent's argument to make it easier to attack ("My opponent wants to abolish all police, leaving us defenseless!" when they actually proposed police reform). This allows for a perceived victory without addressing the real issue.
- **Appeal to Emotion:** Manipulating an emotional response in place of a valid argument ("If you don't support this policy, you don't care about our children!"). This bypasses rational System 2 processing.
- **Bandwagon Fallacy (Ad Populum)**: Asserting that a claim is true or good simply because many people believe it or do it ("Everyone knows that our way is the best way; millions agree!"). This reinforces tribal

identity and cohesion by suggesting that the in-group's beliefs are inherently correct due to their popularity within the group or wider society.

- **Appeal to Authority (Fallacious):** Asserting that a claim is true because an authority figure (who may not be an expert in that specific field) says it is true, or using an authority figure as the sole basis for an argument ("Dr. X says this treatment works, so it must be true!" when Dr. X is a celebrity, not a medical expert). This can be used to leverage a respected figure within the tribal identity to shut down debate.

- **False Dilemma/Dichotomy (Black-or-White Fallacy):** Presenting only two options or outcomes as the only possibilities, when in fact there are more ("Either you're with us, or you're with the terrorists!"). This forces individuals to choose sides, reinforce tribal loyalty, and eliminate the possibility of nuance or alternative solutions.

- **Slippery Slope:** Asserting that a relatively small first step will inevitably lead to a chain of related, usually negative, events that culminate in a significant, undesirable outcome ("If we allow X to happen, then Y will surely follow, and soon Z will destroy everything!"). This taps into fear and can be used to prevent any deviation from the status quo or in-group norms.

- **Hasty Generalization:** Drawing a broad conclusion based on a small or unrepresentative sample of evidence ("I met two rude people from that city, so everyone from there must be unfriendly!"). This can reinforce negative stereotypes about out-groups or generalize a single negative experience to dismiss an entire opposing viewpoint.

- **Appeal to Ignorance (Ad Ignorantiam):** Arguing that a claim must be true because it has not been proven false, or false because it has not been proven true ("No one has proven ghosts don't exist, so they must be real!"). This shifts the burden of proof and can be used to maintain a belief in the absence of evidence, often to protect a comfortable worldview.

- **Red Herring:** Introducing irrelevant information or a side issue to distract from the main argument ("You're questioning my tax plan? What about the rampant crime in our streets?"). This deflects criticism and diverts attention from weaknesses in one's own position, protecting ego or policy.
- **Tu Quoque ("You Also" aka What-about-ism):** Attempting to discredit an opponent's argument by pointing out that they have acted inconsistently with their own argument or made similar mistakes in the past ("You're telling me to stop smoking, but you used to smoke too!"). This defends against criticism by deflecting blame, implying hypocrisy rather than addressing the substance of the argument.
- **Begging the Question (Circular Reasoning):** The premise of an argument assumes the truth of its conclusion, essentially arguing in a circle ("God exists because the Bible says so, and the Bible is true because God wrote it"). This serves to reinforce an already held belief within a tribal context, making it seem self-evidently true.
- **No True Scotsman:** Redefining the group or category in order to exclude a counter-example to a generalization ("No true environmentalist would ever drive an SUV!" in response to someone who is an environmentalist but drives an SUV). This protects the integrity of the in-group's definition and maintains ideological purity against inconvenient counterexamples.
- **Genetic Fallacy:** Judging something as good or bad based on where it comes from, or from whom it comes, rather than on its own merits ("That idea came from a socialist country, so it must be bad!"). This immediately dismisses ideas based on their origin from an out-group, reinforcing tribal prejudice.
- **Burden of Proof:** Stating that the burden of proof lies with the person who is denying or questioning the claim ("Prove that aliens don't exist!"). This forces the opponent to disprove a negative, making it difficult to

challenge an unsupported assertion and protecting the speaker's claim from scrutiny.

- **Appeal to Nature:** Arguing that something is good, right, or acceptable because it is "natural" or "unnatural" ("Eating meat is natural, so it's perfectly fine"). This can be used to justify practices or beliefs based on a simplified understanding of what is "natural," often serving to defend traditional or tribal practices.

- **Personal Incredulity:** Because one finds something difficult to understand or believe, they conclude it's not true ("I can't imagine how evolution could create such complex life, so it must be false"). This prioritizes one's own limited understanding over evidence, often to protect a comforting worldview or belief system.

These logic fallacies, as defense mechanisms utilized by our underlying optimizers, are powerful tools for evasive thinking, diversion tactics, and obfuscation, both for ourselves and others. They protect our internal coherence and social standing, even at the cost of truth.

We often employ what are called psychological defense mechanisms to navigate the complexities of reality, protect ourselves from anxiety, and maintain a stable self-image. These unconscious strategies, first extensively theorized by Sigmund Freud and later elaborated upon by his daughter Anna Freud, serve as mental filters that distort, deny, or otherwise manipulate reality to reduce emotional distress arising from internal conflicts or external threats. While essential for coping with stress and trauma in the short term, their overuse or rigid application can prevent individuals from confronting and resolving underlying issues. This can lead to maladaptive behaviors and a distorted perception of the world. Understanding these mechanisms offers insight into the hidden ways our minds protect us, often without our conscious awareness. But make no mistake, these are vulnerabilities that can be exploited.

Common Defense Mechanisms

- **Repression:** The unconscious blocking of unacceptable thoughts, feelings, or memories from conscious awareness. For example, a person might not remember a traumatic childhood event.
- **Denial:** The refusal to accept reality or a fact, acting as if a painful event, thought, or feeling does not exist. For instance, an alcoholic refusing to admit they have a drinking problem.
- **Projection:** Attributing one's own unacceptable thoughts, feelings, or impulses to another person. For example, a person who is habitually late accusing their punctual colleague of being unorganized.
- **Displacement:** Redirecting emotions, usually anger, from the original source to a substitute target that is less threatening. For instance, yelling at your spouse after a bad day at work instead of confronting your boss.
- **Rationalization:** Explaining an unacceptable behavior or feeling in a rational, logical manner, avoiding the true explanation for the behavior. An example is someone failing an exam and saying, "I didn't really want to pass that class anyway."
- **Reaction Formation:** Expressing the opposite of one's true feelings or impulses in a highly exaggerated way. For example, a person who unconsciously dislikes their boss becoming overly friendly and complimentary towards them.
- **Regression:** Reverting to an earlier, more childish, and less mature stage of development when faced with stress or anxiety. An example is an adult throwing a temper tantrum when they don't get their way.
- **Sublimation:** Channeling unacceptable impulses or feelings into socially acceptable and often productive activities. For instance, a person with aggressive tendencies becoming a successful boxer or surgeon.
- **Intellectualization:** Focusing on the intellectual components of a stressful situation, rather than the emotional aspects, to avoid feeling

distressed. For example, a doctor discussing a patient's terminal illness using detached medical jargon, avoiding emotional connection.
- **Identification:** Adopting the characteristics, beliefs, or behaviors of another person or group, often a powerful or admirable one, to enhance one's self-esteem or reduce anxiety. For example, a child who has been bullied at school starting to bully younger children.

Motivated Reasoning

Expanding on the concept introduced in Chapter 1, motivated reasoning is the unconscious tendency of individuals to process information in a way that allows them to reach a desired conclusion. This means our reasoning is biased by our goals or desires. Research by Ziva Kunda (1990) demonstrated that when people are motivated to arrive at a particular conclusion, they are more likely to seek out evidence that supports it and dismiss evidence that contradicts it.

The dangerous truth is that in the modern information environment, where access to data is ubiquitous, increased information can paradoxically drive people *further* from the truth when non-truth-seeking optimizers (ego, tribal, belief preservation, worldview, fear, prejudice, self-interest) are dominant. Instead of using new information to refine understanding, it is selectively cherry-picked to reinforce existing biases and conclusions. For example, someone deeply committed to a political ideology might encounter a news report that contradicts their view. Rather than consider its validity, their tribal identity optimizer might prompt them to immediately dismiss the source as biased or fake, thus solidifying their original belief. The contradictory information may even be seen as proof itself that the "other side" will stop at nothing to subvert the "truth". Motivated reasoning, therefore, employs defense mechanisms, cognitive biases, and even intentional fallacy use (rather than mere shortcuts) to serve its underlying purpose.

Conspiratorial Thinking

The human mind, in its quest for understanding and control, is remarkably adept at pattern recognition. However, this very strength can become a significant cognitive vulnerability, especially when faced with complexity, uncertainty, or a perceived lack of control. This vulnerability is often exploited by, and contributes to, the widespread appeal of conspiratorial thinking.

People are drawn to conspiracy theories for many reasons. At an epistemic level, they offer seemingly definitive and straightforward explanations for confusing or overwhelming events, satisfying our inherent need for understanding and cognitive closure. A complex disaster or a sudden political shift can be deeply unsettling, and the idea of a secret, malevolent plot, while alarming, can feel more coherent and manageable than random chance or a multitude of chaotic factors. It provides a narrative that "makes sense," even if it's based on flimsy evidence or outright fabrication.

It is useful to differentiate between real-life conspiracies (for example, Watergate or the Iran-Contra affair, which were later proven by evidence) and conspiratorial thinking, which are often elaborate, unsubstantiated narratives attributing malevolent plots to powerful groups. The psychological underpinnings of why individuals adopt and cling to conspiracy theories are complex.

What are some of the psychological underpinnings of conspiratorial thinking?

- **Need for Control and Meaning:** In times of uncertainty or crisis, conspiracy theories offer simple, coherent explanations and restore a sense of control where events might otherwise feel random or overwhelming. They satisfy our brain's drive to construct stories and impose order.

- **Distrust of Authority:** Erosion of trust in institutions such as government, media, and science creates fertile ground for alternative narratives. Conspiracy theories thrive where skepticism of official accounts turns into outright rejection.
- **Confirmation Bias:** Once adopted, conspiratorial beliefs are reinforced by confirmation bias. Supporters seek out "evidence" that fits the theory and dismiss contradictory facts as part of the cover-up, creating a self-sealing worldview.
- **Motivated Reasoning:** Belief in a conspiracy can optimize for different psychological needs: feeling special through "hidden knowledge" (ego optimizer), affirming a political stance or group loyalty (tribal identity optimizer), or alleviating fear by simplifying a complex world (anxiety optimizer).
- **Need to Belong:** Beyond individual motives, conspiracy theories also serve powerful social needs. They provide a sense of community, shared identity, and solidarity, especially for those who feel marginalized. The "us versus them" framing reinforces group cohesion while offering belonging and purpose.

Conspiracy thinking, therefore, is a powerful delusion driver, capable of warping an individual's reality and making them profoundly susceptible to further manipulation.

Beyond the need for understanding, existential motives play a role. In times of crisis, powerlessness, or heightened anxiety, conspiracy theories can offer a sense of agency or control. If a powerful, hidden group is responsible for adverse events, then at least there's a discernible cause, and perhaps, a means to resist or prepare. This can be more comforting than confronting the unsettling reality of random misfortune or systemic issues that feel too vast to tackle. Blaming an easily identifiable "other" can also serve as a psychological defense, deflecting discomfort from personal responsibility or the complexities of reality.

Furthermore, social motives strongly fuel conspiratorial thinking. Believing in a conspiracy can foster a powerful sense of belonging and identity within a group that "knows the truth." This forms an exclusive in-group, often united by a shared distrust of official narratives or out-groups. The act of uncovering "hidden knowledge" can lead to feelings of intellectual superiority or special insight, boosting self-esteem. This tribal reinforcement, amplified by echo chambers in modern communication, creates a reinforcing loop where shared beliefs, no matter how unfounded, solidify group bonds and resist contradictory evidence. The optimizers work to ensure informational alignment and create a model that cannot be refuted. This is a sort of self-induced epistemic cult.

Ultimately, falling into conspiratorial thinking is a cognitive vulnerability because it often stems from a combination of motivated reasoning outside the goals of truth and the strategic utilization of cognitive shortcuts. Our brains, seeking efficiency and comfort, can readily accept compelling narratives that confirm existing biases or alleviate anxieties, even when those narratives lack robust evidence and lead to a distorted, often paranoid, view of the world.

Brain States and Triggering Mechanisms

Our cognitive landscape is not static; it shifts and adapts based on internal and external cues. We can think of different brain states as distinct modes of operation for our minds, each with its own set of active optimizers, cognitive biases, and framing. These states can be "triggered" by specific cues from others, the environment, or even ourselves.

Consider a public policy discussion. Ideally, participants would operate in a "discovery and innovation" brain state, activating truth optimizers, engaging System 2 thinking, and collaboratively seeking optimal solutions. However, a single loaded word, a perceived slight, or a rhetorical framing that taps into "us vs. them" narratives can instantly trigger a "fight for your tribe and identity" brain state. In this state, tribal identity optimizers seize control. The discussion rapidly devolves from rational deliberation to a contest of loyalty and opposition. Talking points and what-about-isms fly back and forth. Facts become irrelevant, and the goal shifts from finding truth to defending the in-group and attacking the out-group. This illustrates precisely how tribalism and identity, once triggered, can profoundly override truth-seeking rational thought, leading directly to the delusions that often characterize deeply polarized societies.

CHAPTER 3
Mind Viruses and Social Contagion

"Misinformation or distrust of vaccines can be like a contagion that can spread as fast as measles."
- Theresa Tam

Just as biological viruses spread through populations, certain ideas, beliefs, and behaviors can spread and replicate through minds, transforming thoughts and actions. This phenomenon is often described through the concept of cognitive viruses, also known as mind viruses or memes. Coined by Richard Dawkins in his 1976 book *The Selfish Gene*, a "meme" (analogous to a "gene") is a unit of cultural information, such as an idea, belief, pattern of behavior, or style, that is transmitted from one mind to another. These "mind viruses" can be anything from catchy jingles to political slogans, conspiracy theories, or even moral values. They propagate through communication, imitation, and learning, essentially "infecting" minds and shaping collective thought. The more "fit" a meme is (meaning it is easily remembered, emotionally resonant, or socially useful), the more likely it is to replicate and spread.

The rapid dissemination of such cognitive viruses is facilitated by social contagion, a well-documented phenomenon in social psychology. Social contagion refers to the spontaneous spread of emotions, behaviors, and ideas through a group or network. For example, researchers have observed the contagious nature of yawning, laughter, and even risk-taking behaviors in crowds. On a broader scale, studies by Nicholas Christakis and James Fowler have shown how phenomena like obesity, smoking cessation, and even happiness can spread through social networks, extending to friends of friends of friends. This spread is not just about direct influence but about observational learning, mimicry, and the subtle pressures of social norms. When a new idea, especially one that evokes strong emotions, takes root within a social circle, it can quickly cascade through the entire network, often bypassing individual critical evaluation.

In the digital age, social contagion is dramatically amplified, leading to the formation of echo chambers and filter bubbles. An echo chamber occurs when a person is exposed only to information and opinions that reinforce their existing beliefs, often due to social connections that share similar views. A filter bubble, a term coined by Eli Pariser, is a personalized intellectual isolation that results from algorithms on platforms like social media and search engines, which selectively guess what information a user would like to see based on past activity. Both phenomena create self-reinforcing loops that limit exposure to diverse perspectives and solidify existing beliefs, leading to ideological insulation. Within these insulated environments, cognitive viruses can spread unchecked, gaining legitimacy through repetition and social proof, and making it increasingly difficult for individuals to encounter or accept contradictory evidence. The lack of exposure to differing viewpoints can lead to more extreme positions and a diminished capacity for empathy towards those outside the bubble.

Central to the power of mind viruses and social contagion is the role of emotion. Strong emotions like fear, anger, anxiety, and even excitement can significantly bypass rational thought and critical processing. Research in neuroscience demonstrates that highly emotional stimuli can lead to a "fight or flight" response, diverting cognitive resources away from the prefrontal cortex (responsible for System 2 thinking) and towards more primitive, reactive brain regions. This makes individuals far more susceptible to manipulation. When a cognitive virus is packaged with an emotionally charged narrative (for example, a conspiracy theory that exploits fear of an "other," or a political message designed to evoke outrage), it gains immense persuasive power. The emotional arousal can override the individual's critical thinking, leaving them vulnerable to accepting information that, under calmer circumstances, they might question. Emotions act as a fast lane for ideas, allowing them to penetrate our cognitive defenses before System 2 has a chance to engage.

The Thought Terminating Cliché

A thought-terminating cliché is a seemingly simple phrase or saying that, upon closer inspection, serves to shut down critical thinking and debate. Rather than encouraging deeper consideration of an issue, it provides a pre-packaged, easily digestible "answer" that discourages further inquiry or dissent. The term was coined by Robert Jay Lifton in his 1961 book, *Thought Reform and the Psychology of Totalism: A Study of "Brainwashing" in China*, where he observed their use in totalitarian regimes to suppress independent thought.

How a Thought-Terminating Cliché is a Cognitive Vulnerability

Thought-terminating clichés represent a significant cognitive vulnerability because they exploit our natural tendencies towards cognitive ease, conformity, emotional resonance, stopping dissent, and belief reinforcement.

- **Cognitive Ease**
  Our brains prefer to conserve energy, and these clichés offer a quick, low-effort explanation that bypasses the more demanding process of critical analysis. They provide an illusion of understanding without requiring real engagement.

- **Conformity and Social Cohesion**
  Often, these clichés are widely accepted within a group or society. Challenging them can feel like challenging the group itself, leading to social discomfort or ostracism. This pressure to conform can override individual critical thinking.

- **Emotional Resonance**
  Many thought-terminating clichés carry an emotional charge, often appealing to values like patriotism, common sense, or tradition. This emotional appeal can bypass rational thought, making the cliché seem self-evidently true.

- **Suppression of Dissent**
  By providing a readily available "answer," these clichés effectively shut down further discussion or alternative viewpoints. They create an intellectual dead end, preventing exploration of nuances, complexities, or dissenting opinions. This makes individuals more susceptible to manipulation and less capable of independent judgment.

- **Reinforcement of Existing Biases**
  Thought-terminating clichés often align with pre-existing biases or stereotypes, further entrenching them rather than encouraging a re-evaluation of one's own assumptions.

Thought-terminating clichés act as mental shortcuts that lead to intellectual cul-de-sacs, preventing the kind of deep, nuanced thinking necessary for robust decision-making and resistance to manipulation. They are a product of one of the non-truth-seeking strategic optimizers being activated. They leave individuals open to being swayed by simplistic arguments and less equipped to navigate complex realities. Thought-terminating clichés often are turned into memes (especially online).

Examples of Thought-Terminating Clichés

- **Political/Social**
  - "It is what it is." (Discourages questioning the status quo or seeking solutions.)
  - "That's just common sense." (Dismisses alternative perspectives as illogical or ignorant.)
  - "You're either with us or against us." (Forces a binary choice, eliminating nuance or neutrality.)
  - "Freedom isn't free." (Used to justify various actions or sacrifices without further debate.)
  - "If you don't like it, move." (Shuts down criticism of a system or country.)
  - "Fake news." (A blanket dismissal of any information that challenges a belief.)
  - "We need to get back to basics." (Often a vague appeal to nostalgia that avoids specific policy discussions.)
- **Business/Workplace**
  - "Think outside the box." (Often used to encourage innovation without providing concrete methods or resources.)
  - "It's just good business." (Justifies an action without ethical or long-term consideration.)
  - "There's no 'I' in team." (Can be used to suppress individual initiative or dissent.)
  - "Synergy." (A buzzword that often lacks concrete meaning but sounds positive.)
- **Personal/Motivational**
  - "Everything happens for a reason." (Can discourage active problem-solving or accountability for negative events.)
  - "It's all part of God's plan." (Similar to the above, can lead to passivity.)

- o "Just tough it out." (Discourages seeking help or addressing underlying issues.)
- o "Look on the bright side." (Can invalidate legitimate negative feelings or concerns.)

These clichés, while seemingly innocuous, can subtly yet powerfully undermine critical thought, making individuals more susceptible to influence and less capable of independent judgment. Recognizing them is the first step in mitigating their impact as a cognitive vulnerability.

Dietrich Bonhoeffer's Theory of Stupidity and Social Contagion

The susceptibility to mind viruses and the power of social contagion are perhaps nowhere more chillingly illuminated than in Dietrich Bonhoeffer's reflections on what he called "stupidity". Bonhoeffer, a German theologian and anti-Nazi dissident, wrote about the nature of stupidity while imprisoned during World War II. His observations, though rooted in a specific historical context, offer profound insights into a cognitive vulnerability that can be deeply exploited by mind viruses and amplified by social contagion.

Bonhoeffer argued that stupidity is not primarily an intellectual defect, but rather a moral one. Stupidity is also a type of social contagion. He posited that stupid people are often not unintelligent; in fact, he noted that many highly intelligent individuals can become astonishingly stupid when they are part of a sufficiently powerful and uncritical group. For Bonhoeffer, stupidity is less about a lack of intellect and more about a lack of independent judgment, a willful refusal to engage with facts, and an uncritical acceptance of prevailing narratives. This is especially true for those promoted by an embraced authority.

He observed that stupidity is more dangerous than malice because it cannot be reasoned with. Against malice, one can protest; against stupidity, arguments are useless. The stupid person is impervious to facts and rational argument because their thinking is not based on reason but on an unquestioning adherence to a pre-approved set of ideas or slogans. This is where the link to social contagion becomes acutely clear.

Bonhoeffer's theory suggests that stupidity is often a socially contagious condition. When an individual becomes part of a large, cohesive group that shares a particular mind virus – be it a political ideology, a conspiracy theory, or a simplistic worldview – they can become "stupidified." This process occurs through groupthink, emotional surrender, defense against dissent, and the "protective coating".

- **Groupthink and Conformity**
  As highlighted in the discussion of cognitive ease and conformity, individuals within a group susceptible to social contagion often prioritize fitting in over critical thinking. Bonhoeffer noted that stupidity often arises when individuals, fearing isolation or disagreement, surrender their independent judgment to the group's dominant narrative. The "stupid" individual, in this context, is not necessarily lacking in personal intelligence, but rather has allowed their intelligence to be subsumed by the collective.

- **Emotional Surrender**
  The chapter already emphasizes the role of emotion in bypassing rational thought. Bonhoeffer's "stupid" person is often driven by emotions like fear, anger, or loyalty to the group, which are easily manipulated by emotionally charged mind viruses. These emotions short-circuit critical evaluation, making the individual highly receptive to simplistic, emotionally resonant messages.

- **Defense Against Dissent**
    Bonhoeffer noted that the stupid person becomes an unwilling tool of evil, often defending the group's agenda with fervor, even when it is demonstrably false or harmful. This aligns with the "suppression of dissent" aspect of thought-terminating clichés. The "stupid" person, infected by a mind virus and reinforced by social contagion, actively (though unknowingly) suppresses any information that challenges the group's belief system.

- **The "Protective Coating"**
    Bonhoeffer described stupidity as a kind of "protective coating" that shields individuals from confronting uncomfortable truths or inconvenient facts that might challenge their cherished beliefs or the group's narrative. This "coating" is reinforced by echo chambers and filter bubbles, where the individual is constantly fed information that validates their existing mind virus, making it almost impossible for contradictory evidence to penetrate.

Bonhoeffer's theory of stupidity describes a critical vulnerability within the human cognitive models that is amplified by the scaling mechanisms of social contagion. It illustrates how the spread of mind viruses, particularly those packaged as thought-terminating clichés or memes, can lead otherwise intelligent individuals to abandon their capacity for independent thought and critical analysis. This transformation from rational individuals to "stupid" participants in a collective delusion underscores the profound danger that unchecked cognitive viruses and robust social contagion pose to both individual well-being and societal health. The individual, caught in the grip of such a contagion, becomes less an independent thinker and more a conduit for the replication of the "stupidifying" memes.

CHAPTER 4
Digital Age Amplification of Cognitive Vulnerabilities

"The problem with the internet is that it's a giant echo chamber where everybody is saying the same thing to each other."
- Brian Eno

The vulnerabilities inherent in the human mind, sculpted over millennia, have found a new and unprecedented amplifier in the digital age. Technologies that connect us globally also expose us to cognitive threats on an unimaginable scale.

The most obvious and impactful amplifier is social media and scale. Social media platforms have fundamentally transformed how information is disseminated. Unlike traditional media, where content undergoes editorial review, social media allows anyone to publish anything to potentially billions of people instantly. This accelerates the spread of information, and critically, misinformation, to unprecedented scales. A false rumor or a doctored image can go viral globally in minutes, reaching millions before any attempt at correction can be made. The sheer volume and velocity of information overload our cognitive systems, pushing us further into System 1 processing and making us more susceptible to the biases discussed in Chapter 1. The algorithmic design of these platforms, which prioritizes engagement (often driven by emotional content), inadvertently or intentionally amplifies polarizing and sensational material.

While the internet promised a global village, it has also delivered a niche for everyone. The ability of the internet to connect individuals with highly specific interests and beliefs, no matter how niche or extreme, has led to a fragmentation of our shared reality. If you are interested in a specific hobby, a particular historical interpretation, or even a fringe scientific theory, the internet can connect you with thousands, if not millions, of like-minded individuals. While this fosters community and diverse interests, it also allows individuals to self-select into highly insulated echo chambers (as discussed in Chapter 3), solidifying existing beliefs and making cross-ideological discourse increasingly rare and difficult. This hyper-specific targeting creates a perfect breeding ground for niche cognitive viruses to thrive, reinforced by a dedicated and isolated audience.

The Printing Press

To understand the profound, digital revolution induced societal shifts occurring today, it is useful to consider a Historical Parallel: The Printing Press. The invention of the movable-type printing press in the 15th century by Johannes Gutenberg similarly disrupted society by decentralizing information. Before the printing press, knowledge was largely controlled by institutions like the church and universities, and information spread slowly through handwritten manuscripts. The printing press democratized access to information, leading to the protestant reformation, the Scientific Revolution, and the Enlightenment. However, it also led to an explosion of printed material, fueling religious wars and new forms of ideological conflict. The printing press fundamentally changed the information-based power structure, shifting from an oral/scribal culture to a print culture, demanding new ways of processing information and evaluating truth.

Drawing parallels to the current digital age, we see a similar pattern of disruption. Just as the printing press broke the monopoly on information, the internet has fragmented traditional media and authority structures. This decentralization has empowered individuals and movements but also unleashed unprecedented levels of misinformation and ideological polarization. The cognitive demands of navigating a print-saturated world were immense for medieval people. The cognitive demands of navigating a digitally saturated, algorithmically curated world are even more immense for modern people.

The digital age has accelerated both globalization and fragmentation. While technology has brought the world closer, it has not necessarily led to greater understanding or homogeneity. Instead, studies, such as those by Samuel Huntington on the clash of civilizations or Robert Putnam's work on social capital and diversity, explain mechanisms and motivations that lead people to differentiate and solidify their identities in a globalized world. This often results in increased fragmentation rather than cohesion. When exposed to a vast global landscape of diverse cultures and ideas, people often react by emphasizing their unique identity and bonding more tightly with those who share it. This can be seen in the rise of nationalism, religious fundamentalism, and identity politics across the globe. Rather than dissolving differences, globalization can paradoxically highlight and reinforce them, feeding into the tribal instincts we discussed earlier. The digital platforms, through their global reach, amplify these differentiation processes, allowing people to find and reinforce increasingly specific in-groups. This has further fragmented collective understanding and created fertile ground for cognitive attacks that target these fault lines. In part two, we will shift our focus from our cognitive vulnerabilities to how these vulnerabilities are exploited.

PART II
The Exploitation of Our Minds' Vulnerabilities

CHAPTER 5
The Art of Manipulation – From Persuasion to Coercion

*"The best way to manipulate a man
is by making him think he is a master of his own destiny."*
– Unknown

Having explored the inherent vulnerabilities of the human mind, we now turn our attention to the deliberate and often sophisticated ways these weaknesses are exploited. Manipulation is the art of influencing others, not through rational argument or open negotiation, but by subtly leveraging cognitive biases, emotional responses, and psychological predispositions to achieve a desired outcome. This spectrum ranges from ethical persuasion to outright coercion, with many shades of grey in between.

At its milder end, manipulation often relies on well-established Principles of Persuasion, extensively researched by social psychologist Robert Cialdini and others. His foundational work, particularly in *Influence: The Psychology of Persuasion*, outlines six key principles. These principles are reciprocity, consistency, social proof, authority, liking, and scarcity.

- **Reciprocity**
  People are more likely to comply with requests from those who have previously given them something. This creates a sense of obligation. (Example: A free sample at a grocery store makes you more likely to buy the product.)

- **Commitment and Consistency**
  Once people make a small commitment, they are more likely to follow through with larger, consistent actions. (Example: Signing a small petition makes you more likely to donate to the cause later.)

- **Social Proof**
  People look to others to determine what is correct, especially when uncertain. (Example: "Millions of satisfied customers!" or a crowded restaurant implies quality.)

- **Authority**
  People tend to obey legitimate authority figures, even if the requests are questionable. (Example: White lab coats in commercials lend credibility to product claims.)

- **Liking**
  People are more easily persuaded by those they like, whether due to shared interests, compliments, or physical attractiveness. (Example: Salespeople who build rapport or mirror your body language.)

- **Scarcity**
  Opportunities seem more valuable when their availability is limited. (Example: "Limited time offer!" or "Only X items left!")

Beyond Cialdini's work, modern marketing and political campaigns employ advanced psychological insights to fine-tune these principles.

Moving to a more organized and large-scale form of influence, psychological operations (PsyOps) and propaganda represent deliberate attempts by governments, militaries, or organizations to influence the attitudes and behaviors of target audiences. Historically, propaganda has been used in wartime to demoralize enemies or rally domestic support, often employing simplistic narratives, emotional appeals, and demonization of "the other." Think of World War II posters or Cold War rhetoric. These posters were basically memes. In the modern age, PsyOps leverage advanced data analytics, social media, and psychological profiling to deliver highly targeted messages. These targeted messages are designed to shape public opinion, recruit sympathizers, or sow discord within an adversary's ranks. The goal is not just to convey information but to manipulate perceptions, often by exploiting existing biases and vulnerabilities.

The core of effective manipulation lies in exploiting cognitive biases discussed in Chapter 1. Manipulators do not need to understand neuroscience; they need only observe predictable human behavior.

Examples of Manipulation:

- **Confirmation Bias:** A political campaign might strategically disseminate only information that confirms the existing biases of a target demographic, creating a reinforced echo chamber and preventing exposure to opposing viewpoints.
- **Anchoring Effect:** A car salesperson might start with an artificially high price for a vehicle, making subsequent, slightly lower prices seem like a great deal, even if they are still above fair market value.
- **Framing Effect:** News outlets can frame identical events differently to elicit specific emotional responses and political alignments from their audiences. For example, reporting unemployment figures can focus on "job losses" or "people finding new opportunities," depending on the desired narrative.

These practical, real-world examples illustrate how specific biases are intentionally leveraged in marketing (to increase sales), politics (to win votes), and social engineering (to gain access or information).

In the digital realm, a particularly insidious form of exploitation emerges: Dark Patterns. Coined by UX designer Harry Brignull, dark patterns are deceptive user interface designs that trick users into unintended or harmful actions. These are not accidental design flaws but intentionally crafted to exploit cognitive vulnerabilities and psychological principles.

Digital Exploitation Examples:

- **"Roach Motel"**: Easy to get into, hard to get out of (e.g., subscription services with complex cancellation processes). This exploits the commitment and consistency bias.
- **"Privacy Zuckering"**: Tricking you into sharing more personal information than you intend (e.g., confusing privacy settings that default to public sharing).
- **"Confirmshaming"**: Guilt-tripping users into opting into something they might not want (e.g., "No thanks, I prefer to pay full price" as the only alternative to a discount offer).

Dark patterns exploit our inherent desire for convenience, tendency to skim rather than read carefully, and aversion to extra effort, leading us to unwittingly give away data, spend more money, or sign up for unwanted services.

CHAPTER 6
Self-Exploitation and Delusion

*"The first principle is that you must not fool yourself—
and you are the easiest person to fool."*
- Richard Feynman

While the previous chapters explored how external actors manipulate our cognitive vulnerabilities, the most insidious forms of exploitation often come from within. In their relentless drive for coherence, efficiency, and self-preservation, our brains can inadvertently become the architects of our own delusion. This isn't about conscious deception, but rather the subtle, powerful ways our internal "optimizers" (as discussed in Chapter 1) twist reality to serve needs other than objective truth. This chapter explores the landscape of self-exploitation, revealing how we ourselves can trigger our vulnerabilities and construct elaborate mental strongholds to protect comforting falsehoods.

The Inadvertent Trigger

Recall the strategic optimizers introduced in Chapter 1: Ego, Tribal Identity, Belief, Worldview, Fear, Prejudice, and Self-Interest. These are powerful, often subconscious, algorithms guiding our reasoning. Some optimizers, like the "discovery" or "truth" optimizers, which motivate us to reason towards objective reality, can be easily overridden, leading to self-exploitation.

Consider a simple debate. You might begin with a genuine desire to understand or share information. However, in your excitement, you exaggerate a study or piece of evidence to make a point. When challenged by someone, the fear of losing face and being embarrassed may initiate the ego optimizer. The goal shifts from seeking truth to being *right* and saving face. You might find yourself committed to exaggerating points, dismissing valid counterarguments, or even fabricating details to win the argument. This is self-exploitation in action, where our internal systems prioritize emotional comfort and perceived social standing over intellectual integrity.

The Self-Fulfilling Prophecy

One of the forms of self-exploitation is a concept called the self-fulfilling prophecy. This is a prediction that, by being made, actually causes itself to become true. It's not about mystical foresight, but about how our beliefs and expectations subtly, and sometimes not-so-subtly, influence our behavior and, consequently, the outcomes we experience.

The concept was famously articulated by sociologist Robert K. Merton in 1948, building on the work of W. I. Thomas, who stated, "If men define situations as real, they are real in their consequences." Essentially, our initial, often unfounded, belief about a situation or person can lead us to act in ways that elicit reactions confirming that very belief.

A Manager Named Sarah

Imagine a new manager, Sarah, who holds an unconscious belief that her team members are inherently resistant to change. This belief, though unfounded, triggers a "fear optimizer" within her, leading to a defensive mindset. She might then inadvertently communicate new initiatives with an overly cautious and confrontational tone, anticipating resistance. Her team, picking up on her unpalatable communication style, might indeed become more resistant and uncooperative, thus "confirming" Sarah's initial belief.

What started as an internal cognitive bias becomes an externalized reality, manufactured by Sarah's own actions driven by her internalized belief system.

The danger lies in the feedback loop: the "confirmed" prophecy further entrenches the initial belief, making it even harder to dislodge. Our brains interpret the outcome as evidence for the initial belief, reinforcing the self-exploitation cycle and hindering objective reality testing.

Echo Chamber of the Mind

Confirmation bias can be a type of self-exploitation. It's the pervasive tendency to seek out, interpret, favor, and recall information in a way that confirms one's pre-existing beliefs or hypotheses, while giving disproportionately less consideration to alternative possibilities.

As a *realized exploit*, confirmation bias turns our own minds into self-perpetuating echo chambers. Instead of critically evaluating new information, our brain's belief optimizers spring into action. We may gravitate towards news sources, social media accounts, and conversations that validate what we already think. We may twist neutral or ambiguous information to fit our narrative. We may remember information that supports our beliefs more readily than contradictory evidence. We may even find reasons to discount or ignore anything that challenges our cherished views, often labeling it "fake news" or "biased".

The impact is that instead of converging on truth as we encounter more information, confirmation bias can drive us *further* from it. This self-inflicted insulation hardens our beliefs, making us less capable of rational discourse and more vulnerable to external manipulators who simply feed us what we already want to hear.

The Mind's Imperative for Internal Peace

As we learned earlier, cognitive dissonance, the psychological discomfort arising from holding two or more conflicting beliefs, values, or attitudes, is a powerful internal trigger. When our behavior contradicts one of our own beliefs, or when new information clashes with our established worldview, our strategic optimizers help us to reduce this inconsistency.

Our brain's intense drive to avoid cognitive dissonance often leads to self-deception rather than genuine change or growth. It's often easier to change the facts in our head than to rewrite our identity or fundamental beliefs. For instance, someone who deeply identifies as an environmentally conscious individual but frequently takes long-haul flights might rationalize their behavior by arguing that their individual impact is negligible, or that technological solutions will eventually solve climate change, rather than reducing their travel. This self-generated justification alleviates the discomfort without requiring a change in behavior or a fundamental re-evaluation of their identity. The mind compartmentalizes the inconsistency, creating blind spots that prevent us from seeing our own contradictions.

Mistaking Familiarity for Understanding

We live in a world of unprecedented complexity, yet our brains are wired for efficiency, not perfect, detailed understanding. This leads to the "illusion of explanatory depth," where we vastly overestimate our understanding of how complex systems work. We think we grasp economics, climate science, political systems, or even simple everyday objects (like how a zipper works) far better than we actually do.

This false confidence is a critical vulnerability for self-exploitation. Because we *feel* like we understand, we are more susceptible to simplistic narratives, vulnerable to conspiracy theories, and less likely to seek genuine expertise.

Being more susceptible to simplistic narratives means complex problems become reducible to easy "good vs. evil" stories, often offered by charismatic leaders or ideological movements.

The vulnerability to conspiracy theories increases when reality is messy and uncertain. A conspiracy theory offers a seemingly coherent, albeit fabricated, explanation that feels satisfying and complete, tapping into our storytelling brain's desire for meaning.

We are often less likely to seek genuine expertise since: why consult an expert when we already "know" how it works?

The core issue is that we mistake familiarity with understanding. We can recognize the terms and perhaps explain a few surface-level mechanics, but we lack a deep causal understanding. Our System 1 provides a quick, satisfying "feeling of knowing," and our System 2, being lazy, often uncritically endorses this illusion. This prevents deeper inquiry and leaves us open to manipulation by those who exploit this superficial comprehension. Our own self-exploitation leads to others being able to exploit us even further.

The Paradox of Ignorance

As we learned in chapter 1, the Dunning-Kruger Effect, which was first documented by psychologists David Dunning and Justin Kruger, is a cognitive bias where individuals with low ability at a task overestimate their own ability, while high-ability individuals often underestimate theirs. This phenomenon is particularly dangerous because the less we know, the louder and more confidently we preach it, making us more invested in our flawed understanding.

This increased investment activates non-truth-seeking optimizers. An inflated sense of competence makes us resistant to feedback or contradictory evidence. Our strategic optimizers solidify our incorrect understanding because admitting error would mean a blow to our self-image. The cycle is self-reinforcing: perceived expertise (even if unfounded) leads to vocal pronouncements, which increase commitment to the belief, further activating optimizers that shut down self-correction. This can lead intelligent individuals astray, transforming confident ignorance into a barrier against genuine learning and critical thought.

The Smarter We Are, The Better We Are at Lying to Ourselves

Paradoxically, intelligence can sometimes amplify self-exploitation. Highly intelligent individuals are often remarkably adept at rationalization. They can construct elaborate, seemingly logical justifications for beliefs they hold for non-truth-seeking reasons (e.g., tribal loyalty, self-interest, emotional comfort). They are better at building defenses around their cherished delusions.

This isn't to say intelligence is a hindrance, but rather that it can be weaponized *by our own internal optimizers*. When a tribal identity optimizer is operating, an intelligent person can weave a more convincing, complex narrative to defend their group's position. This is the case even if it's based on flawed premises, making them less likely to be swayed by simple facts. The brain's capacity for complex thought, when directed by motivated reasoning, becomes a tool for self-deception and basically self-exploitation of one's own cognitive vulnerabilities.

The Preference for a False Story Over Chaos

As discussed with "the storytelling brain" (Chapter 2), our minds are relentless meaning-makers. We crave causality and coherence. When faced with incomplete information, ambiguity, or contradictory experiences, the chaos drives our innate storyteller to step in and weave a narrative that imposes order and provides a sense of understanding.

This means we'd rather have a false, simple story than a true, complicated one. A clear, satisfying (even if fabricated) narrative alleviates cognitive discomfort and provides the illusion of control. This cognitive bias is a driver of delusion. For example, a complex economic downturn might be better explained by a confluence of global factors, but our brains often prefer a simpler story: "It's the fault of X group" or "It's a deliberate plot by Y." This gives us a clear "villain" and a digestible explanation, satisfying our need for meaning, even if it's objectively untrue.

When "Common Sense" Becomes Collective Delusion

Our tribal instincts (Chapter 1) are a powerful driver of self-exploitation. We are deeply social creatures, and belonging to a group has immense evolutionary advantages. This deep-seated need leads us to outsource our beliefs to the group and call it "common sense".

When we are part of a cohesive group, the "tribal identity optimizer" can become highly active. We may prioritize group cohesion and loyalty over individual accuracy. This manifests as conformity, social proof (everyone knows), and thought-terminating clichés.

The danger is that this common sense is often nothing more than a shared delusion, amplified within an echo chamber. Individuals become less independent thinkers and more conduits for the replication of group-sanctioned mind viruses. The group's narrative dictates judgment, even when it contradicts objective reality.

The Endowment Effect

The endowment effect that we learned about in chapter 1 describes our tendency to disproportionately value something once we own it, simply because we own it.

The Endowment Effect extends beyond physical possessions to our ideas, opinions, and even memories. Once an idea or belief becomes "ours" and even more so, once we've publicly expressed it, defended it, or integrated it into our identity, we will value it more highly. This can trigger one of our non-truth strategic optimizers.

Letting go of a belief feels like a loss, not just a correction of an error. This perceived loss activates the loss aversion heuristic (our tendency to react more strongly to potential losses than gains), making us cling tighter to our cherished convictions, even in the face of contradictory evidence. Our brains resist the disinvestment from an idea that has become part of our belief system.

Self-Deception as a Survival Mechanism - When Evolution Goes Wrong

At its core, much of self-exploitation is rooted in self-deception, which, paradoxically, evolved as a survival mechanism. In ancestral environments, being able to genuinely believe our own advantageous (but not strictly true) narratives could offer benefits. Such as increased confidence, where believing in one's own superior abilities (even if slightly exaggerated) could lead to bolder actions and greater success in competition for mates or resources. Self-deception could also reduce stress by denying harsh realities or minimizing threats, which could reduce anxiety, allowing for more adaptive responses. Another evolutionary adaptation is group cohesion, where a shared, comforting narrative, even if partially false, could foster stronger group bonds and collective action.

An individual might genuinely believe they are a better hunter than they are, leading them to pursue game more confidently, which occasionally (through sheer effort) leads to success, reinforcing the belief. Or a group might believe in a protective deity, which fosters courage in battle.

However, in the modern world, these adaptations could become vulnerabilities for self-exploitation and delusion.

The benefits of self-deception are often outweighed by risks in the modern world:

- **Blindness to genuine threats:** Denying the reality of climate change or a personal health issue, while comforting in the short term, can lead to catastrophic long-term consequences.
- **Resistance to learning and adaptation:** If we are always 'right' in our own minds, we stop learning and adapting to new information, which is required in this fast-changing technological world.
- **Fueling collective delusion:** When self-deception is shared and reinforced across a group, it can lead to widespread societal delusions, making rational discourse and collective problem-solving nearly impossible. This may lead to global instability, which we all now rely on.

Our evolved capacity for self-deception, in some ways an adaptive tool for navigating a dangerous and uncertain world, can also be seen as a self-exploit, enabling our descent into personal delusion in a new world environment where objective truth is needed for survival.

CHAPTER 7

Cybercrime and Perils of the Digital World

*"It is easier to manipulate a man
who doesn't believe he can be fooled than it is to fool him directly."*
- Nassim Nicholas Taleb

The digital world is a fertile ground for the exploitation of cognitive vulnerabilities, where malicious actors leverage our psychological predispositions for financial gain, data theft, or other illicit purposes. The methods are often sophisticated, preying on universal human tendencies.

Scams and frauds are perhaps the most direct application of cognitive exploitation. Con artists, whether operating online or offline, instinctively understand and exploit universal cognitive weaknesses like trust, urgency, and fear.

What are some common scams?

- **Phishing:** As discussed with the "Urgent Payroll Update" example in Chapter 1, phishing emails or messages create a sense of urgency and threat, bypassing System 2 thinking by triggering fear optimizers. They often mimic trusted authorities (banks, IT departments) to leverage the authority bias.
- **Romance Scams:** These prey on loneliness and the deep human need for connection, building trust and emotional attachment over weeks or

months before asking for money. They exploit the liking bias and the emotional attachment to beliefs.
- **Grandparent Scams:** These leverage fear and love for family, with a scammer impersonating a grandchild in distress, needing immediate money for an emergency. The urgency and emotional appeal override skepticism.
- **Tech Support Scams:** These scams often begin with a pop-up message appearing on a user's screen, claiming their computer is infected with a virus or has a critical error. The message usually mimics legitimate security warnings and creates a sense of urgency and fear. It instructs the user to call a toll-free number for "technical support." Once the user calls, a scammer, impersonating a technician, will try to convince them to grant remote access to their computer, purchase unnecessary software or services, or pay for "repairs" that aren't needed. They exploit the authority bias (posing as legitimate tech support) and fear (of computer damage or data loss).
- **Online Shopping Scams (Fake Websites/Products):** Scammers create sophisticated fake e-commerce websites or listings on legitimate platforms (like social media marketplaces) offering highly desirable products at unbelievably low prices. These sites often look professional, sometimes even mimicking well-known brands. Once a purchase is made, the consumer either receives a counterfeit item, a much cheaper item than what was ordered, or nothing at all. They exploit the desire for a good deal (scarcity, urgency, "too good to be true" offers) and the liking bias (attractive product images, professional-looking website).
- **Investment Scams (Ponzi, Crypto Scams):** These scams promise high, guaranteed returns with little to no risk, often involving speculative investments like cryptocurrency or foreign exchange trading. Scammers use professional-looking websites, impressive-sounding jargon, and fabricated testimonials to build credibility. They may even show initial "returns" to encourage victims to invest more and to recruit

others. Eventually, the scheme collapses, and investors lose their money. They exploit the desire for wealth, greed, and the authority bias (presenting themselves as financial experts). The pressure to "get in now" before an opportunity is gone also leverages urgency.

- **Lottery/Sweepstakes Scams:** Victims receive an unsolicited email, letter, or phone call congratulating them on winning a large sum of money in a lottery or sweepstakes they never entered. To "claim" their winnings, they are told they must pay an upfront fee for taxes, processing, or customs. Of course, no winnings exist, and the fee goes directly to the scammer. They exploit hope, greed, and the desire for an easy windfall. The demand for an upfront fee leverages urgency ("act now to claim your prize!").
- **Job Scams:** These scams target individuals looking for employment, often advertising highly attractive positions with excellent pay and benefits that require little experience or effort. After applying, victims may be asked to pay an "upfront fee" for training, background checks, or equipment. Alternatively, they might be asked to provide sensitive personal and financial information (like bank account details for direct deposit) that is then used for identity theft. They exploit the need for income, hope, and the desire for convenience (work-from-home opportunities). They leverage urgency by suggesting the position is in high demand.
- **"Pig Butchering" Scams (Advanced Fee Fraud with Relationship Building):** This is a sophisticated blend of romance scams and investment scams. The scammer first builds a long-term relationship with the victim, often posing as a romantic interest. Once trust is established, they introduce an "investment opportunity," typically in cryptocurrency or a similar high-yield scheme. The initial "investments" might show impressive (fake) returns, encouraging the victim to invest more and more, sometimes even taking out loans. Eventually, the scammer disappears with all the money. This deeply exploits loneliness,

the desire for connection, trust, and greed, combining the emotional manipulation of romance scams with the financial lure of investment fraud.

These scams work not because victims are unintelligent, but because they are human, equipped with brains wired for social connection and immediate threat response, rather than constant suspicion.

Beyond financial scams, a more sinister form of coercion, a ransomware of the mind, is emerging. This involves coercing individuals through intense psychological pressure, often leveraging personal data or emotional leverage. Unlike traditional ransomware that encrypts data, this targets the mind directly.

Ransomware of the Mind Examples

- **Doxing and Extortion:** Threatening to release sensitive personal information (medical records, embarrassing photos, private communications) unless a ransom is paid. This exploits fear of social ruin or legal repercussions.
- **Emotional Blackmail:** Manipulating relationships and deep-seated emotional bonds to force compliance, often seen in abusive relationships or cults (which we will explore further).
- **Gaslighting:** Systematically undermining a person's perception of reality, making them doubt their own memories, sanity, or judgment. This erodes a person's cognitive independence and makes them highly susceptible to the manipulator's narrative.

These methods aim to isolate the victim and break down their trust in their own cognitive processes, making them entirely dependent on the exploiter.

The individuals who most effectively perpetrate these schemes often exhibit traits associated with the dark triad in exploitation, which include Machiavellianism, Narcissism, and Psychopathy.

- **Machiavellianism:** Characterized by a manipulative, cynical, and calculating approach to others. Individuals high in Machiavellianism are adept at identifying and exploiting the vulnerabilities of others for their own gain.
- **Narcissism:** Marked by grandiosity, a sense of entitlement, and a lack of empathy. Narcissists often exploit others for admiration or personal advantage, seeing others as mere extensions of themselves.
- **Psychopathy:** Defined by a lack of empathy, impulsivity, superficial charm, and antisocial behavior. Psychopaths are skilled at deception and often feel no remorse for exploiting others.

Cognitive Attack Vectors

Just as cybersecurity professionals map technical weaknesses in systems to understand potential attack paths, malicious actors, instinctively or through deliberate study, perform a similar vulnerability mapping of the human mind. They identify inherent cognitive biases and psychological needs, then systematically exploit them through tailored attack vectors. Let's explore some common cognitive vulnerabilities and adversaries' tactics and techniques to leverage them, mirroring the systematic approach of frameworks like the MITRE ATT&CK matrix used in cybersecurity.

Tactic: *Initial Access* -> Gaining a Foothold in the Mind

The initial phase focuses on establishing a connection and trust, or creating an immediate, undeniable need for action.

- *Vulnerability*: **Trust & Social Reciprocity**
    - **Description:** Humans are predisposed to trust others, especially those perceived as familiar, authoritative, or in need of help. We also feel a subconscious obligation to reciprocate favors or perceived kindness.
    - **Techniques:**

- **Impersonation (Authority/Familiarity):** Posing as a trusted entity (bank, IT support, family member, government agency) or a peer.
  - *Examples:* Phishing emails from "your bank," fake tech support pop-ups, or "grandparent" scam calls.
- **Pre-texting/Role-Playing:** Creating a believable, fabricated scenario or persona to extract information or manipulate actions.
  - *Examples:* Romance scammer building a fake life story, or job scammer outlining a dream role.
- **Establishing Rapport:** Spending time building a friendly or empathetic connection to foster a sense of obligation.
  - *Examples:* Extensive conversations in romance scams, or "friendly" tech support agent.
- **Offering Assistance/Value:** Providing something seemingly beneficial (e.g., "free" security scan, investment tip) to trigger reciprocity.
  - *Examples:* Fake antivirus offers in tech support scams, or initial "small wins" in investment scams.

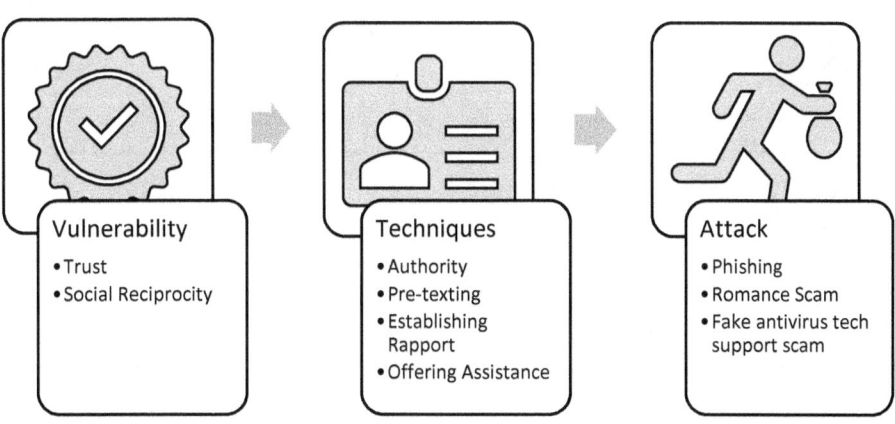

Cognitive Attack Surface | 77

- *Vulnerability*: **Urgency & Fear of Loss**
  - **Description:** Our System 1 thinking is highly reactive to perceived threats or time-sensitive opportunities, bypassing deeper critical analysis. The fear of missing out (FOMO) or suffering a loss is a powerful motivator.
  - **Techniques:**
    - **Threat/Imminent Danger:** Presenting an immediate negative consequence if action isn't taken.
      - *Examples:* "Your account will be suspended," "Your computer is infected," or "Your grandchild is in jail."
    - **Time-Sensitive Offer/Deadline:** Creating a limited window for action to prevent careful consideration.
      - *Examples:* "Act now to claim your prize," or "This investment opportunity won't last."
    - **Scarcity:** Implying limited availability of a desirable item or opportunity.
      - *Examples:* "Only 3 items left at this price" on a fake shopping site, or an exclusive investment "invite."

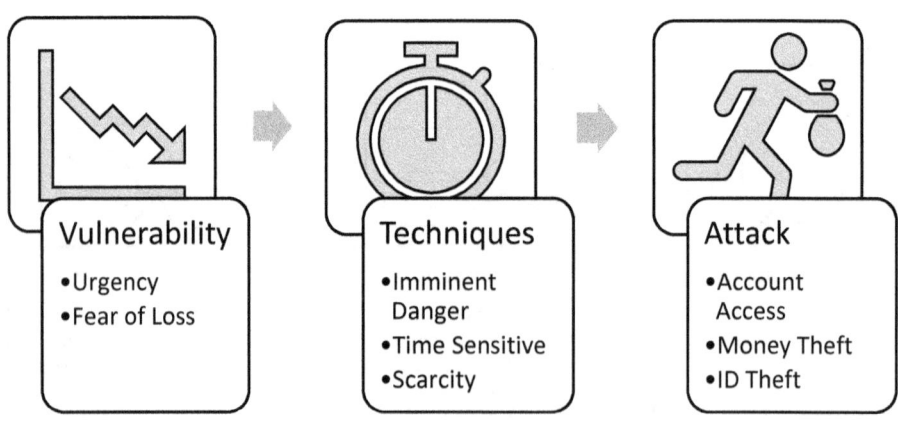

Tactic: *Execution & Manipulation* -> Guiding the Victim's Actions

Once a foothold is established, the adversary guides the victim through a series of actions that lead to the desired outcome (e.g., money transfer, data disclosure).

- *Vulnerability*: **Authority Bias & Obedience**
    - **Description:** A tendency to comply with instructions from perceived authority figures, even if those instructions seem questionable.
    - **Techniques:**
        - **Command & Control:** Directing the victim through a series of steps, often with explicit instructions.
            - Examples: Tech support instructing the victim to download software, or an "IRS agent" demanding payment over the phone.
        - **Legitimizing with Jargon/Logos:** Using official-sounding terminology, branding, or mimicking legitimate communication channels.
            - *Examples:* Fake bank websites with accurate logos, or investment scams using complex financial terms.
        - **Threat of Non-Compliance:** Implying negative consequences for not following instructions (e.g., legal action, further technical issues).
            - *Examples:* "If you don't pay, the police will be involved," or in grandparent scams, "Your warranty will be voided."

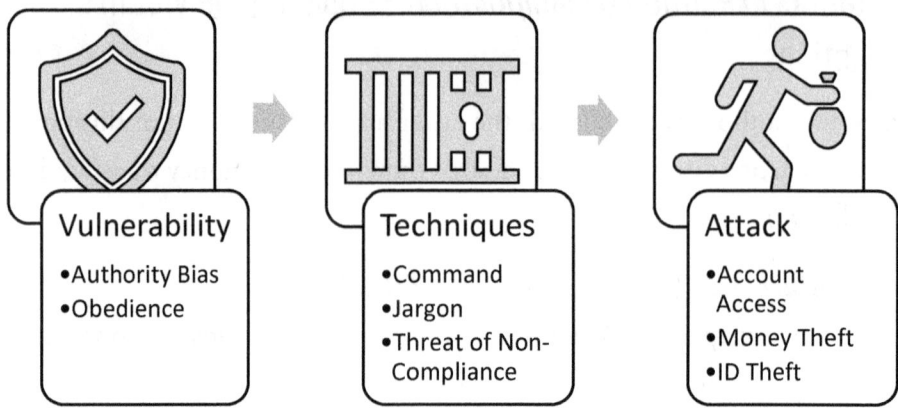

- *Vulnerability*: **Greed & Desire for Gain**
    - **Description:** The innate human desire for personal benefit, wealth, or advantage.
    - **Techniques:**
        - **Promise of High Returns:** Advertising unrealistic profits or windfalls.
            - *Examples:* "Double your money in a week" in crypto scams, or lottery winnings.
        - **Exclusive Opportunity:** Presenting an offer as unique or only available to a select few.
            - *Examples:* "Special investment opportunity just for you," or "secret shopping deals."
        - **Low Effort/High Reward:** Implying significant benefits with minimal personal investment or work.
            - *Examples:* "Work from home, earn $5000 a week," job scams, or an easy lottery claim process.

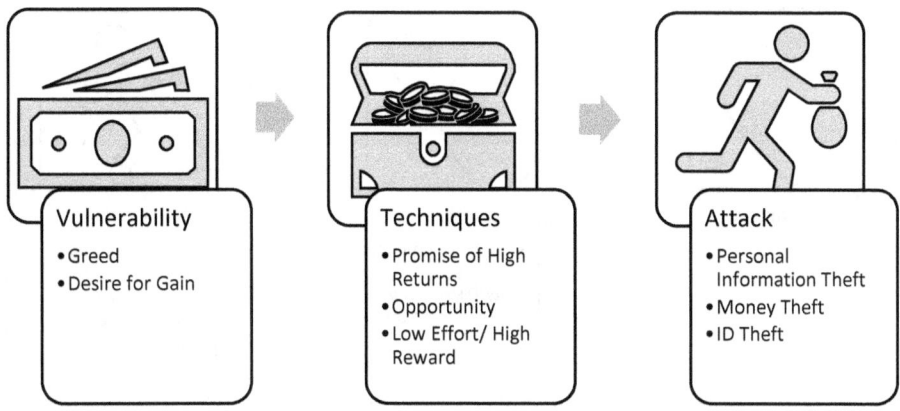

- *Vulnerability*: **Loneliness & Emotional Needs**
    - **Description:** The fundamental human need for connection, affection, and belonging.
    - **Techniques:**
        - Emotional Attachment Building: Spending extended periods developing a deep emotional bond.
            - *Examples:* Long-term messaging and calls in romance scams, or "pig butchering" scams.
        - **Pity/Distress Stories:** Fabricating crises or hardships to elicit sympathy and financial aid.
            - *Examples:* Romance scammer needing money for a "medical emergency," or grandparent scammer in "jail."
        - **Validation & Flattery:** Providing compliments, attention, and affirmations to boost the victim's self-esteem and attachment.
            - *Examples:* Constant praise and declarations of love in romance scams.

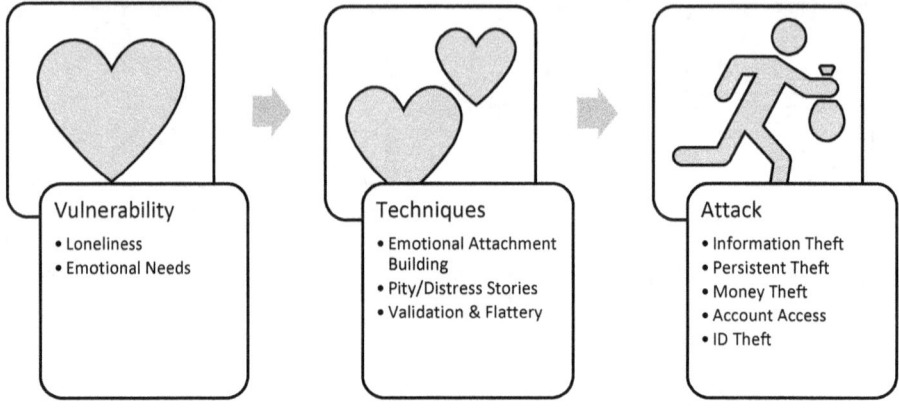

Tactic: *Defense Evasion & Persistence* -> Maintaining Control and Preventing Discovery

These tactics aim to prevent the victim from realizing they are being scammed or from seeking external help.

- *Vulnerability*: **Confirmation Bias & Cognitive Dissonance**
  - **Description:** The tendency to seek out and interpret information in a way that confirms existing beliefs, and to avoid information that contradicts them, even in the face of evidence.
  - **Techniques:**
    - **Reinforcing Narratives:** Continuously providing "evidence" or stories that support the scam's legitimacy.
      - *Examples:* Fake investment dashboards showing "returns," or elaborate explanations for delays or problems.
    - **Discrediting External Advice:** Convincing the victim to distrust friends, family, or official warnings.
      - *Examples:* "Don't tell anyone, they won't understand," or "Your bank is trying to stop you."

- **Isolation:** Encouraging the victim to keep the relationship or investment secret.
  - *Examples:* Romance scammers demanding secrecy, investment scams emphasizing "confidentiality."

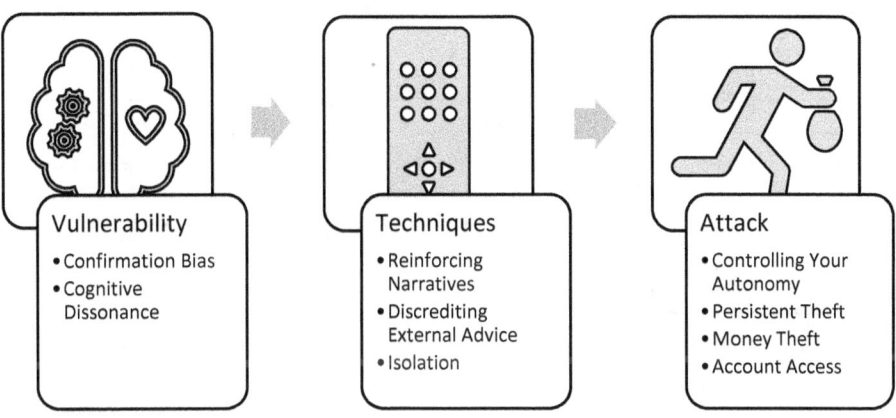

- *Vulnerability*: Self-Preservation & Shame
  - **Description:** The desire to protect one's reputation, avoid embarrassment, or prevent negative personal consequences.
  - **Techniques:**
    - **Doxing/Extortion:** Threatening to expose sensitive or embarrassing information.
      - *Examples:* Ransomware of the Mind for embarrassing photos or private communications.
    - **Shame & Blame:** Making the victim feel responsible or foolish if they don't comply or try to back out.
      - *Examples:* "You'll lose everything if you pull out now," or "You promised me."
    - **Gaslighting:** Systematically manipulating the victim's perception of reality to make them doubt their own judgment.

- *Examples:* Denying past conversations, or making the victim believe they are forgetful or irrational.

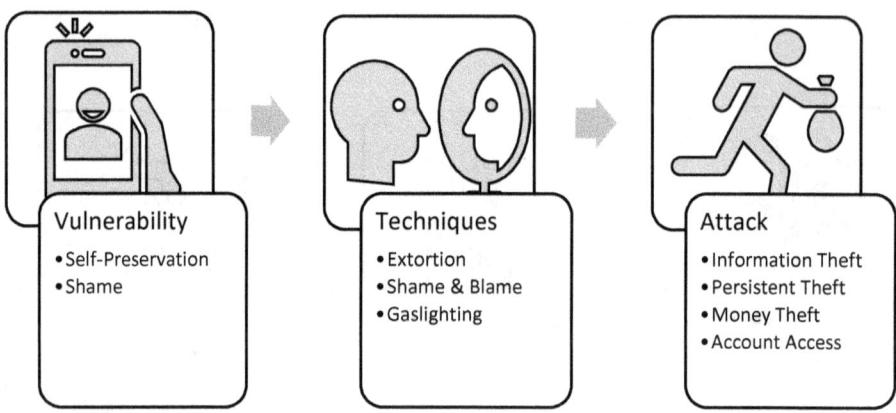

- *Vulnerability*: **Overwhelm & Cognitive Load**
    - **Description:** When faced with too much information, complex instructions, or rapid demands, System 2 thinking can become fatigued, leading to reliance on System 1 shortcuts.
    - **Techniques:**
        - **Information Overload:** Bombarding the victim with complex details, technical jargon, or multiple simultaneous requests.
            - *Examples:* Rapid-fire instructions during a tech support call, or dense legal-sounding documents for fake investments.
        - **Rapid Pacing:** Rushing the victim through decisions or actions.
            - *Examples:* "You need to do this *now*," pressuring for quick money transfers.
        - **Multiple, Conflicting Instructions:** Intentionally creating confusion to make the victim more reliant on the scammer's "guidance."

- *Examples:* Tech support giving confusing steps, then "taking over" the computer.

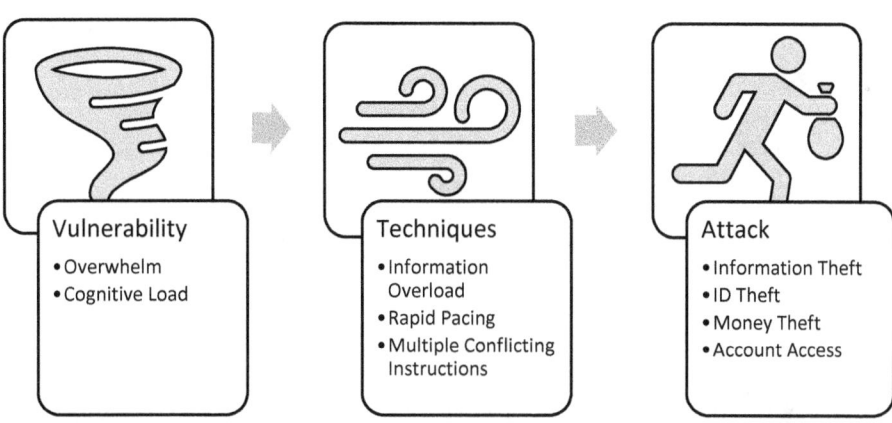

These pervasive scams work not because victims are unintelligent, but because they are human, equipped with brains wired for social connection, immediate threat response, and efficiency, rather than constant suspicion and exhaustive critical analysis. Just as a cybersecurity expert maps an information system's weaknesses, these malicious actors understand (sometimes instinctively) the "entry points" into the human mind, such as a person's need for belonging, fear of loss, desire for certainty, or inherent trust. They then craft tailored "attack vectors" (scams, narratives, emotional appeals) to exploit these specific vulnerabilities, maximizing their chances of success. They understand that the easiest path to manipulation is often through the victim's cognitive vulnerabilities.

CHAPTER 8

Cults, Extremism, and the Erosion of Critical Thinking

"When a man is a part of a mass, his mental faculties are dulled, and he is incapable of original thought."
- Carl Jung

The most profound and systematic exploitation of cognitive vulnerabilities often culminates in phenomena like cults and extremist movements. These environments are designed to dismantle individual autonomy and replace it with a collective, usually delusional, reality.

Cult Dynamics

Cult dynamics are the tactics of indoctrination, isolation, thought reform, and the systematic dismantling of individual autonomy. Cults thrive by exploiting fundamental human needs such as the desire for belonging, meaning, security, and definitive answers in a complex world. The process often involves five key components, which are love bombing, isolation, thought reform, and dismantling autonomy.

- **Love Bombing**
  New recruits are overwhelmed with affection and attention, creating a powerful sense of immediate belonging and validation (exploiting liking and social proof).

- **Isolation**
  Gradually, recruits are separated from their existing support networks (family, friends, outside information) to ensure the cult's narrative becomes their sole source of reality. This weakens the ability to cross-reference or receive critical feedback.

- **Thought Reform (Brainwashing)**
  Through repetitive indoctrination, sleep deprivation, controlled information, and peer pressure, critical thinking is systematically eroded. Complex ideas are simplified into dogmatic slogans, and dissent is punished.

- **Dismantling Autonomy**
  Individuals are encouraged to surrender their personal judgment and decision-making to the leader or group, leading to a profound sense of dependence and a complete adoption of the cult's worldview.

- **"Us vs. Them" Mentality**
  The cult establishes a rigid in-group/out-group dynamic, demonizing external critics and reinforcing the idea that only the cult possesses the "truth." This taps into deeply wired tribal optimizers.

Research by psychologists like Margaret Singer and Steven Hassan, who have worked extensively with former cult members, details the devastating cognitive and emotional impact of these practices.

Closely related to cult dynamics is radicalization, the psychological pathways and stages that lead individuals to embrace extremist ideologies, whether online or offline. This is a process of intense ideological conversion, often driven by a cocktail of personal grievances, a desire for significance, and exposure to compelling narratives. This process typically happens through four distinct stages.

The Four Stages of Radicalization

1. **Pre-radicalization:** Individuals may feel disenfranchised, isolated, or seek meaning.
2. **Self-identification:** They encounter an extremist ideology that seems to offer answers or a sense of belonging.
3. **Indoctrination:** They immerse themselves in the ideology, often in echo chambers, reinforcing beliefs and demonizing opponents.
4. **Action:** They become committed to acting on the ideology, sometimes violently.

This process heavily leverages tribalism and identity, offering a clear "us vs. them" framework and a powerful new identity tied to the cause. It's important to differentiate between hate speech, which explicitly promotes violence or discrimination against a group, and legitimate opinion, even if that opinion is controversial or strongly held. However, extremist groups exploit the fine line, often couching hate speech as "free speech" to gain a foothold and normalize their views. The tolerance paradox, as theorized by philosopher Karl Popper, highlights the dilemma of being tolerant of the intolerant. Absolute tolerance can lead to the disappearance of tolerance itself when intolerant ideologies are allowed to flourish unchecked. It is a moral imperative of those who embrace tolerance to reject intolerance. Often, an exploiter will slowly prepare potential victims who embrace tolerance with emotional manipulation, making their extreme views seem more normalized.

Grooming

An insidious form of exploitation, particularly in online spaces, is grooming. This refers to the deliberate process of preparing individuals for exploitation, control, or abuse, often leveraging trust and emotional manipulation over time. While usually associated with child exploitation, grooming tactics are used by various malicious actors, including recruiters for extremist groups.

It involves building a relationship, identifying vulnerabilities, and gradually normalizing harmful ideas or behaviors, slowly dismantling the victim's defenses until they become compliant.

Purity Culture

Purity culture, often rooted in conservative religious teachings (particularly evangelical Christianity), creates an environment ripe for victim-blaming and abuse through several interconnected mechanisms. The four primary mechanisms are the objectification of women, rape culture, secrecy, and increased vulnerabilities.

1. **Objectification and Devaluation of Women and Girls**
    - Shame and Guilt -> Purity culture often teaches that a woman's value is tied to her virginity or "purity." If she is not "pure" (meaning she has engaged in any sexual activity outside of a very narrow definition, usually heterosexual marriage), she is considered "damaged," "used," or "defiled." This instills deep shame and guilt, making individuals feel inherently flawed or unworthy.
    - Responsibility for Male Behavior -> A core tenet is that women are responsible for men's sexual thoughts and actions. This manifests in teachings about modesty (dressing to avoid "tempting" men) and "sexual gatekeeping," where women are expected to control both their own and men's sexual urges. This shifts the blame for male predatory behavior onto women.
    - Diminished Bodily Autonomy -> Women's bodies are often presented as not truly their own, but rather something to be "preserved" for a future husband or for God. This denies them agency over their own sexuality and physical selves.
2. **Creation of a "Rape Culture" Environment**
    - Victim Blaming -> When sexual assault or abuse occurs, purity culture's emphasis on female responsibility can lead to victims being

blamed for the assault. Questions like "What were you wearing?" or "Why were you there?" implicitly or explicitly suggest the victim was at fault for "tempting" the perpetrator or failing to "guard their purity."

- Minimization of Consent -> Purity culture often lacks comprehensive sexual education, notably regarding consent. The focus is on abstinence and avoiding "sin," rather than on healthy boundaries, mutual respect, and enthusiastic consent. This can leave individuals ill-equipped to identify or prevent non-consensual acts.
- Perpetrator Excuses -> By portraying men as having uncontrollable sexual urges, purity culture can inadvertently provide an excuse for abusive behavior. The narrative implies that men "can't help themselves," thereby absolving them of full responsibility for their actions and shifting the burden onto women to prevent being "tempted."

3. **Silence and Secrecy, Facilitating Abuse**
    - Culture of Silence -> Sex and sexuality are often taboo subjects outside of very specific, often shame-filled, contexts within purity culture. This makes it incredibly difficult for victims of abuse to speak up, as they may fear further shame, judgment, ostracization from their community, or being seen as "impure" themselves.
    - Protection of Perpetrators -> The emphasis on maintaining a "good" image within the community, combined with the shame associated with sexual matters, can lead to a systemic cover-up of abuse. Institutions and individuals may prioritize protecting the reputation of the community or the abuser over supporting the victim.
    - Internalized Shame -> Victims, having internalized the messages of purity culture, may believe they are "defiled" or "unworthy" after abuse, making them less likely to seek help or report the abuse. They

may feel they are somehow responsible for what happened, preventing them from seeing themselves as a victim.
4. **Mental and Emotional Health Consequences (Increased Vulnerabilities)**
    o <u>Religious Trauma</u> -> The rigid rules, fear-based teachings, and emphasis on shame can lead to religious trauma syndrome, anxiety, depression, and difficulties with body image and sexual identity.
    o <u>Sexual Dysfunction</u> -> Individuals raised in purity culture often struggle with sexual shame and guilt even within marriage, leading to sexual dysfunction, difficulty experiencing pleasure, and strained marital relationships.
    o <u>Distorted Worldview</u> -> Purity culture can create a warped worldview where natural sexual thoughts and desires are deemed sinful, leading to internal conflict and self-condemnation.

Purity culture, while often presented as a means of promoting moral values, can inadvertently create a system where victims of sexual abuse are silenced, blamed, and further traumatized, while abusers may find an environment where their actions are excused or overlooked due to the underlying ideologies.

The Suppression of Dissent

Once individuals are within these controlling ideological systems, the suppression of dissent becomes a commonly used tactic. Mechanisms are used by groups and ideologies to maintain purity of thought and silence opposing viewpoints. This can range from subtle social pressure and shaming to outright censorship, intimidation, and even violence. Any information or perspective that contradicts the group's narrative is labeled as "fake," "enemy propaganda," or "heresy," thereby protecting the collective delusion from external challenge.

As we learned in chapter three, the philosopher Dietrich Bonhoeffer's Theory of Stupidity is particularly insightful here. Bonhoeffer, writing from Nazi Germany, argued that "stupidity is a more dangerous enemy of the good than malice." He contended that stupidity is not primarily an intellectual defect but a moral one, a cultivated resistance to independent judgment in the face of prevailing groupthink. In mass movements, individuals can surrender their critical faculties to a collective will, becoming receptive to any slogans that reinforce the group's agenda, no matter how irrational. This explains how otherwise intelligent individuals can participate in or assent to profoundly irrational or harmful acts when swept up in populist movements, illustrating the dangers of uncritical groupthink.

The Exploitation of Conspiracy Thinking

A pervasive cognitive vulnerability, amplified by the digital age, is conspiracy thinking. In chapter two, we discuss conspiratorial thinking as a delusion driver. The digital age has created an unfortunate golden age for conspiratorial thinking.

How has the digital age amplified conspiratorial thinking?

- **Algorithmic Echo Chambers**
  Social media algorithms are designed to maximize engagement, not truth. This means platforms prioritize content that is emotionally charged, polarizing, or sensational, which feeds conspiracy theories. As users engage with such content, algorithms feed them more of the same, reinforcing beliefs and insulating them from counterarguments.
  Example: Someone who watches a few videos questioning vaccine safety may quickly find their feed flooded with anti-vaccine or broader anti-government conspiracy content, creating a false sense of consensus.

- **Collapse of Traditional Gatekeepers**

  The internet has democratized information, where anyone can publish anything. While this empowers marginalized voices, it also undermines the credibility filtering once provided by journalists, editors, and scholars. In this new landscape, misinformation spreads faster than facts. *Conspiracies can bypass peer review, editorial oversight, and fact-checking entirely.*

- **Rapid Virality and Amplification**

  Digital platforms allow conspiracies to spread at an unprecedented speed and scale. A single post or video can go viral in hours, reaching millions before any fact-check can catch up, which often outpaces the truth.

- **Anonymity and Community Building**

  Online anonymity reduces social consequences for extreme views and allows people to find others who share fringe beliefs. This forms tightly bonded communities with their own norms, jargon, and internal logic, which further reinforces the conspiratorial worldview.

- **Cognitive Bias Magnification**

  The internet heightens confirmation bias, where people seek and trust information that confirms their preexisting beliefs. In digital spaces, individuals can curate their information environments to only include voices that validate their worldview, making belief revision increasingly unlikely.

- **Crisis Amplification**

  In periods of uncertainty, such as with pandemics, political unrest, or economic downturns, there is heightened anxiety and a desire for control. Online spaces become fertile grounds for conspiratorial narratives that offer simple explanations and villains for complex problems.

  "It's not a chaotic pandemic — it's a bioweapon."
  "It's not economic hardship — it's an elite plot."

- **Gamification and Participation**
  Modern conspiracy movements often turn belief into a game. Communities like QAnon encouraged participants to "do their own research" and decode cryptic messages. This active participation makes the belief system more immersive and personally meaningful.
- **Erosion of Trust in Institutions**
  Widespread online misinformation, political propaganda, and the exposure of institutional failures erode public trust in traditional sources of authority. Once that trust breaks down, alternative and even absurd narratives can appear more credible.

The digital age supercharges conspiratorial thinking by enabling rapid spread, emotional manipulation, tribal bonding, and the erosion of truth-seeking norms. It's not just that conspiracy theories are easier to find; they are harder to escape.

The amplification of conspiratorial thinking in the digital age and our cognitive vulnerabilities are actively weaponized by a range of actors, from political operatives to foreign governments to grifters and cult-like movements.

How is conspiratorial thinking exploited?

- **Political Manipulation**
  Authoritarians and populists often promote or exploit conspiracies to:
  - **Discredit opponents** (e.g., "the deep state is sabotaging us"),
  - **Justify power grabs** (e.g., "the election was rigged"),
  - **Rally loyalists** - around a shared enemy, real or imagined.

  Example: Spreading false claims about voter fraud to undermine confidence in democratic processes.

- **Disinformation Campaigns by Foreign Actors**

  Nation-states have run coordinated campaigns to exploit divisions in other countries by seeding conspiracy theories, eroding trust in institutions, and polarizing discourse.

  Example: The Internet Research Agency in Russia created fake social media personas to spread misinformation about vaccines, racial issues, and U.S. elections.

- **Financial Exploitation**

  Grifters exploit conspiratorial communities for profit by selling:
  - "Alternative" health products
  - Prepper gear
  - Conspiracy-themed books and merch
  - Exclusive access to "secret knowledge"

  Example: If someone is convinced the world is being run by a satanic cabal, they'll buy whatever protects them from it.

- **Cult-like Control and Radicalization**

  Some conspiracy movements operate like cults, isolating believers from reality and reshaping their identity. This makes followers more loyal, obedient, and susceptible to manipulation, which may even lead to violence or self-harm.

  Example: QAnon followers have lost family, spent life savings, or participated in crimes, which are all driven by fabricated beliefs.

- **Engagement Farming**

  Influencers, content creators, and media platforms often use conspiratorial content to drive clicks, views, and ad revenue. Conspiracies are sticky, and they provoke outrage, curiosity, and tribal loyalty. All of which translates into digital profit.

- **Undermining Scientific Consensus**

  Anti-science conspiracies (climate denial, anti-vax, flat Earth, etc.) are used to delay regulation, sell pseudoscience, or discredit expert communities. This can serve ideological, political, or economic agendas.

By manufacturing doubt, industries can avoid accountability and regulation even when science is clear.

- **Destabilizing Social Cohesion**
Conspiracy narratives erode shared reality and fracture trust between citizens. This can paralyze collective action, sow paranoia, and lead to extremist outcomes that are sometimes deliberately induced by hostile actors or ideological extremists.

"Divide and conquer" works best when people no longer agree on basic facts.

Exploitation of this vulnerability isn't just accidental; it's a strategic, often lucrative form of manipulation. The same dynamics that make conspiracies appealing also make them powerful tools for control, division, and profit in the hands of bad actors.

CHAPTER 9

Misinformation, Disinformation, and the Information Warfare

"He who controls the past controls the future.
He who controls the present controls the past."
- George Orwell, 1984

In the digital age, information can be used as a tool for enlightenment and a weapon for deception. The landscape has become increasingly dominated by false or misleading content, due to the weaponization of modern communication platforms. We are witnesses to an ongoing global information war. Considering the nuances of this type of modern conflict is useful for understanding how our cognitive vulnerabilities are exploited. But how does modern information war differ from traditional forms of information-based control?

Traditional Propaganda

The goal of traditional propaganda is to influence public opinion, manipulate perception, control behavior, and maintain or gain power (often by governments, political movements, or ideological groups).

Propaganda Strategies

1. **Simplification & Repetition**
    - Use simple messages or slogans, repeated constantly (e.g., "Make America Great Again", or "Yes We Can").

2. **Emotional Appeal**
   o   Trigger fear, pride, anger, or hope to bypass rational thought.
3. **Demonization of the Enemy**
   o   Paint opponents as evil, dangerous, or subhuman.
4. **Patriotic or Moral Framing**
   o   Align the message with national identity, religion, or morality.
5. **Control of Information Channels**
   o   Use state media, censorship, or limited access to counter-narratives.

Propaganda Tactics & Techniques

- **Bandwagon:** Urge people to "join the crowd" because everyone else is.
- **Name Calling:** Attack opponents with negative labels (e.g., "traitor," "terrorist").
- **Glittering Generalities:** Use vague, feel-good language ("freedom," "justice").
- **Transfer:** Associate a respected symbol (e.g., a flag or religious icon) with the message.
- **Card Stacking:** Present only favorable information and suppress the rest.
- **Testimonial:** Use celebrities or respected figures to endorse an idea or ideology.
- **Plain Folks:** Pretend the speaker is "just like you" to gain trust.
- **Scapegoating:** Blame a person or group for broader problems (e.g., immigrants for economic decline).

Traditional propaganda and marketing are both used to influence beliefs, attitudes, or behaviors. While marketing typically promotes products or services for economic gain, propaganda is more often used to push ideological, political, or social agendas. Their strategies and tactics often overlap, drawing from the same toolbox of persuasion techniques rooted in psychology and communication theory. Their evolution into the modern age has seen them adopt more sophisticated data analysis and highly targeted digital distribution.

Traditional Marketing

The goal of marketing is to drive awareness, desire, and action toward a product or service (often by businesses and advertisers).

Marketing Strategies

1. **AIDA Model (Attention, Interest, Desire, Action)**
   - Capture attention → Maintain interest → Build desire → Drive purchase.
2. **Segmentation & Targeting**
   - Tailor messages for specific demographic or psychographic groups.
3. **Unique Selling Proposition (USP)**
   - Focus on what makes the product better or different.
4. **Emotional Branding**
   - Create emotional associations with products (e.g., Coca-Cola = happiness).
5. **Positioning**
   - Shape consumer perception to occupy a distinct place in the market (e.g., Volvo = safety).

Marketing Tactics & Techniques

- **Slogans & Jingles:** Memorable phrases that build brand recognition.
- **Scarcity:** Use limited-time offers or "while supplies last" to create urgency.
- **Social Proof:** Show that others are buying, using, or loving the product.
- **Testimonials & Influencers:** Trusted voices (celebrities, experts) endorse the product.
- **Appeals to Status or Identity:** Buy this to be richer, cooler, more attractive.

- **Repetition:** Familiarity breeds trust—ads run often to reinforce the brand.
- **Visual Branding:** Logos, color schemes, mascots, and packaging to build recall.

Shared Psychological Foundations of Propaganda and Marketing

Both propaganda and marketing tap into:

- **Cognitive biases** (confirmation bias, authority bias, etc.)
- **Heuristics** (mental shortcuts for decision-making)
- **Tribal psychology** (us vs. them framing)
- **Social conditioning** (norms, expectations)
- **Emotional priming** (using emotional cues to influence decisions)

Comparison of Propaganda and Marketing

Propaganda and marketing both aim to influence public perception and behavior, sharing common techniques like repetition, emotional appeal, testimonials, authority, and the use of symbols. However, their core purposes and operational constraints differ significantly. Propaganda primarily focuses on ideological persuasion, often employing high emotional content (such as fear, anger, or pride) and having less constraint on truthfulness, frequently engaging in manipulation. It typically targets a mass or public audience. In contrast, marketing is geared towards commercial promotion, evoking emotions like desire, joy, or trust, and operates within more regulated frameworks, particularly in democratic societies. Marketing also tends to utilize more segmented and niche audience targeting.

Aspect	Propaganda	Marketing
Purpose	Ideological persuasion	Commercial promotion

Aspect	Propaganda	Marketing
Emotional Content	High (fear, anger, pride)	High (desire, joy, trust)
Techniques Shared	Repetition, emotional appeal, testimonials, authority, symbols	Repetition, emotional appeal, testimonials, authority, symbols
Key Difference	Truthfulness is less constrained; often manipulative	More regulated, especially in democratic societies
Audience Targeting	Often mass/public targeting	Often segmented, niche targeting

Propaganda vs. Marketing Chart

The traditional models of propaganda and marketing were primarily utilized by governments and companies on the masses. In the modern world, mass communication has been somewhat democratized, so now we have an added dimension of disinformation campaigns and misinformation spread. This is still utilized by governments and companies, but many other players have entered this arms race.

Before we proceed, we need a clear understanding of the difference between misinformation and disinformation. Misinformation refers to false or inaccurate information that is spread unintentionally. Someone sharing a misleading news article they genuinely believe to be true is spreading misinformation. There is generally no malicious intent (although there are shades of grey here). Disinformation, alternatively, is false information that is deliberately created and disseminated with malicious intent to deceive, manipulate, or cause harm. This includes coordinated campaigns by state actors or extremist groups to spread lies to achieve political or social objectives. But how are disinformation campaigns any different than just propaganda?

Propaganda and disinformation campaigns both aim to influence public perception, but they differ in scope and method. Propaganda is a broad communication strategy that may use truth, half-truths, or lies to shape attitudes and promote a particular agenda, often through emotional appeals and repetition. In contrast, a disinformation campaign is a targeted effort that deliberately spreads false or deceptive information to mislead, confuse, or destabilize. While propaganda can be ideological and long-term, disinformation is always deceptive and often used as a tactical tool within a larger propaganda effort.

Differences Between Propaganda and Disinformation Campaigns

Aspect	Propaganda	Disinformation Campaign
Truthfulness	May include truths, half-truths, or lies	Always includes deliberate falsehoods (intent)
Purpose	Influence perception/behavior	Deceive, destabilize, disrupt
Scope	Broad communication strategy	Targeted misinformation tactic
Methods	Emotional appeal, repetition, symbolism	Fake sources, forged documents, social bots
Examples	Patriotic war posters, ideological messaging	Fake social media accounts spreading false rumors

Propaganda vs. Disinformation Chart

Disinformation campaigns exploit individual vulnerabilities and the tendency to spread misinformation, often by various "bad actors." These campaigns pose a significant global threat. The World Economic Forum Global Risk Report for 2024 now ranks misinformation and disinformation as the number one risk for the next two years.

The State of the World

The 2023 "Freedom on the Net" report by Freedom House, released in October 2023, assesses internet freedom globally. It highlights that global internet freedom declined for the 13th consecutive year, significantly influenced by authoritarian governments leveraging artificial intelligence (AI) to bolster disinformation campaigns while intensifying online censorship. The report found that at least 47 governments deployed commentators to manipulate online discussions in their favor during the coverage period, which is double the number from a decade prior. It also noted the increasing sophistication, accessibility, and ease of use of AI-based tools for generating text, audio, and imagery, leading to an escalation of disinformation tactics. This new technology was utilized in at least 16 countries to sow doubt, smear opponents, or influence public debate. The report emphasizes that AI can amplify digital repression, making censorship, surveillance, and the creation and spread of disinformation easier, faster, cheaper, and more effective. This gives various bad actors incredible leverage.

Disinformation Campaigns by Political Operatives and Parties

Political operatives and parties frequently use disinformation to discredit opponents, manipulate public opinion, or justify political actions. They may spread false claims to undermine confidence in democratic processes, for example, by fabricating voter fraud narratives. Their goal is to solidify their base and demonize opponents by emphasizing "us vs. them" narratives, overriding shared national interests or rational compromise.

Disinformation Campaigns by Foreign Governments/Nation-States

State-sponsored disinformation campaigns are run by foreign actors to sow discord, influence elections, and destabilize other countries. A notable example is the Internet Research Agency in Russia, which created fake social media personas to spread misinformation about vaccines, racial issues, and U.S. elections. According to a 2023 report by Freedom House, over 70 countries experienced government-sponsored disinformation campaigns in the past year, highlighting the pervasive nature of these efforts.

Disinformation Campaigns by Grifters and Opportunists

Individuals or groups exploit conspiratorial communities for financial gain. They sell "alternative" health products, prepper gear, conspiracy-themed books and merchandise, or exclusive access to "secret knowledge". For instance, if someone is convinced the world is being run by a satanic cabal, they are more likely to buy whatever products are marketed to protect them from it.

Disinformation Campaigns by Cults and Extremist Movements

These groups leverage disinformation to recruit new members, maintain control over existing ones, and reinforce their ideological narratives, often leading to extreme behaviors or violence. QAnon followers, for example, have lost family, spent life savings, or participated in crimes, all driven by fabricated beliefs disseminated within the movement. These movements operate like "virtual cognitive cults," offering quick answers, tribal bonding, and a sense of certainty in an uncertain world.

Disinformation Campaigns by Content Creators and Influencers

Driven by engagement metrics, some influencers and media platforms use conspiratorial or sensational content to gain clicks, views, and ad revenue. Conspiracies are "sticky" and provoke outrage, curiosity, and tribal loyalty, all of which translate into digital profit. This means platforms prioritize content that is emotionally charged, polarizing, or sensational, inadvertently or intentionally amplifying such material. Influencers can intentionally or accidentally contribute to populist movements.

Stressed Societies Become Vulnerable to Populist Movements and Disinformation

Populist movements emerge from a society already buckling under economic stress, political disillusionment, and rapid social change. This vulnerability paves the way for a pernicious doom loop. The doom loop starts with an initial susceptibility to populist messaging, creating an opening for disinformation opportunities, which can be effectively exploited in campaigns that further stir social disruption. As disinformation campaigns succeed, they exacerbate societal stress, deepening the underlying vulnerabilities that made the population receptive to divisive rhetoric in the first place. This self-reinforcing cycle continuously fuels the rise of populism and undermines social cohesion.

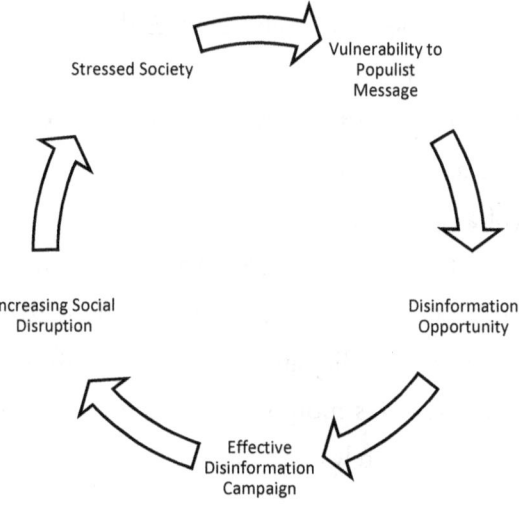

Populist Disinformation Doom Loop

But Why Does Populism Get a Bad Rap? -> The Problem with Most Populist Movements:

- **Us vs. Them Framing:** Populism relies on polarizing narratives: "pure people" vs. "corrupt elites." This can be oversimplified and lead to tribalism, making compromise and pluralism difficult.
- **Erosion of Democratic Norms:** Some populist leaders, once in power, undermine checks and balances, attacking courts, media, or electoral systems, under the guise of fighting corruption or bureaucracy.
- **Emotional Over Rational Appeals:** Populist rhetoric often taps into fear, anger, or nationalism, which can drown out nuanced debate and long-term policymaking.
- **Scapegoating and Xenophobia:** Populism has often used immigrants, minorities, or foreign entities as scapegoats, which can lead to discrimination and violence. It also ignores the underlying issues and is used to mask a populist leader's incompetence.
- **Anti-Expert Sentiment:** Populist movements can delegitimize expertise, such as with scientists, journalists, or economists, claiming they're part of a rigged elite. This can harm policy decisions on climate change, public health, and more. Anti-Intellectualism, by its very nature, is unsustainable since it does not adapt to reality. Without reliable methods to test policy and governance, dysfunction is inevitable. Dysfunction perpetuates more scapegoating and partisan tribalism as populist leaders desperately cling to power.

Disinformation Campaigns by Industries and Special Interest Groups

These actors may spread anti-science conspiracies (e.g., climate denial, anti-vax, flat Earth) to delay regulation, sell pseudoscience, or discredit expert communities, serving their ideological, political, or economic agendas. By manufacturing doubt, industries can avoid accountability and regulation even when scientific consensus is clear. This is especially effective given that the speed of misinformation spread is much faster than fact-checking.

The Speed of Misinformation and Lies

The frightening reality is that false narratives, which are often designed to trigger emotional responses, spread faster and wider than factual corrections. Research done at MIT by Soroush Vosoughi, Deb Roy, and Sinan Aral suggests that false news spreads significantly faster, deeper, and more broadly than the truth on social media, especially on platforms like X (formerly Twitter). Why? False information is often more novel, surprising, and emotionally charged (particularly with anger or fear), making it more engaging and shareable. Truth, conversely, can be mundane, complex, and slow to verify. Malicious actors understand this cognitive vulnerability and intentionally craft emotionally resonant falsehoods that bypass System 2 and activate our primal System 1 responses and underlying optimizers.

Adding another layer of complexity are deepfakes and synthetic media. These are rapidly advancing technologies that blur the lines of reality by using artificial intelligence to generate highly realistic, yet entirely fabricated, images, audio, and video. A deepfake video might show a politician saying something they never said, or an audio clip could perfectly mimic a public figure's voice making a false statement. The cognitive impact of this technology is immense: it erodes trust in visual and audio evidence, which for centuries has been considered reliable. If we can no longer trust our eyes and ears, then the very foundation of empirical reality is shaken, creating a crisis of truth that makes us incredibly vulnerable to any manipulated narrative. Researchers are now studying these digitally-based psychological interactions, such as in cyberpsychology.

Cyberpsychology

Cyberpsychology is a new interdisciplinary field that studies the psychological phenomena that emerge from the interaction between humans and digital technology, especially the internet. It examines how our thoughts, emotions, and behaviors are influenced by online environments, social media, virtual reality, artificial intelligence, and other digital tools.

Cyberpsychology explores how platform design, algorithms, and social dynamics amplify and weaponize cognitive vulnerabilities. Social media platforms are engineered to maximize engagement, often by tapping into our fundamental psychological drives.

Algorithmic Bias and Reinforcement

The algorithms that curate our feeds are designed to show us content we are likely to engage with. This often means reinforcing existing biases. If you interact with content expressing a certain viewpoint, the algorithm will show you more of it, pushing you deeper into an echo chamber. This can unintentionally (or intentionally, in the case of malicious actors) reinforce existing biases and push users towards increasingly extreme content, exacerbating polarization and limiting exposure to diverse perspectives.

Dopamine Loops and Addiction

Social media platforms are expertly designed to exploit our brain's reward system. Each "like," "share," or notification delivers a small hit of dopamine, creating a powerful, addictive feedback loop. This constant craving for social validation and novel stimuli makes users spend more time on platforms, increasing their exposure to information (and misinformation) and making them more susceptible to manipulation. Like any addiction, it can override rational thought and lead to compulsive behavior.

Performance and Identity Shaping

Social media incentivizes the curation of online personas. Users are encouraged to present an idealized version of themselves, leading to constant social comparison and the desire for external validation. This can impact self-perception, leading to anxieties and vulnerabilities related to self-worth, which malicious actors can exploit by offering a sense of belonging or importance through their narratives.

The digital information environment is not a neutral conduit; it is rather an active battleground where our cognitive weaknesses are systematically targeted. However, not all bad outcomes from these vulnerabilities are based on bad intentions. Some platforms, in the interest of fairness, have inadvertently helped misinformation to spread.

Political Asymmetries in Misinformation Enforcement

A study done by Mosleh, Yang, and Zaman, "Differences in misinformation sharing can lead to politically asymmetric sanctions," published in Nature in October 2024, explores why social media platforms might apply policies against misinformation differently across political groups. The researchers, from institutions including MIT Sloan School of Management and the University of Oxford, argue that even if anti-misinformation policies are politically neutral, differences in how various political groups share misinformation can lead to asymmetric enforcement.

The study analyzed data from 9,000 politically active Twitter users during the 2020 US presidential election. It found that users identified as pro-Trump/conservative were substantially more likely to be suspended than pro-Biden/liberal users. Crucially, the study also found that pro-Trump/conservative users shared significantly more links to low-quality news sites, even when news quality was assessed by politically balanced groups of laypeople or groups of only Republican laypeople. This association between conservatism and sharing low-quality news was consistent across seven other datasets from Twitter, Facebook, and survey experiments, spanning 2016 to 2023 and including data from 16 different countries. The authors conclude that these behavioral differences, rather than platform bias, can explain the observed disparities in policy enforcement. People with different political ideologies do not necessarily behave the same way online.

CHAPTER 10
Politicians, Ideology, and the Weaponization of Identity

"The ultimate weakness of violence is that it is a descending spiral, begetting the very thing it seeks to destroy. Instead of decreasing evil, it multiplies it."
- Martin Luther King Jr.

The political arena is a prime example of where cognitive vulnerabilities are expertly exploited, particularly through the strategic manipulation of identity and ideology. Here, the information war transforms into a struggle for the very narratives that define our shared cultural identities.

Political Polarization

Political actors, driven by the desire for electoral gain and power consolidation, expertly exploit identity politics and tribalism. By emphasizing differences between groups ("us vs. them"), they can solidify their base and demonize opponents. This creates deep divisions, where citizens increasingly identify with their political "tribe" above all else, often overriding shared national interests or rational compromise. Research in political psychology consistently shows that party identification can be a stronger predictor of a person's views on an issue than the facts of the issue itself. This is a direct application of the tribal identity optimizers discussed in earlier chapters.

Politicians and grifters are masters of rhetorical devices and fallacies, using language not to enlighten but to manipulate and persuade.

What are some of these tactics?

- **Ad Hominem Attacks:** Instead of debating the policy, a politician might attack the opponent's character or personal history ("You can't trust her economic plan; she's a flip-flopper!"). This distracts from the argument and attempts to discredit the source.
- **Straw Man Fallacy:** Misrepresenting an opponent's argument to make it easier to attack, then refuting the distorted version ("They want to destroy our energy industry and force everyone to ride bicycles!" when the proposal is for clean energy investment).
- **Appeals to Emotion (Fear, Anger, Patriotism):** Bypassing rational deliberation by directly stirring strong feelings. Campaign ads often feature frightening scenarios or evoke intense national pride to sway voters.
- **Slippery Slope:** Asserting that a relatively small first step will inevitably lead to a chain of related, usually negative, consequences (e.g., "If we allow this small regulation, soon the government will control every aspect of our lives!").
- **False Dichotomy (Black and White Thinking):** Presenting only two extreme options as the only possibilities, when in fact more options exist (e.g., "Either you are with us, or you are with the terrorists.").
- **Red Herring:** Introducing an irrelevant topic to divert attention from the original issue (e.g., when asked about a policy failure, a politician might pivot to criticize the media's reporting).

Some others were covered in Chapter 2. By understanding these common tactics, we can better identify when persuasion veers into manipulation.

Manufacturing Consent

The concept of manufacturing consent, famously explored by Edward S. Herman and Noam Chomsky, describes how media and political elites can shape public opinion and gain acquiescence for their agendas. This is not necessarily through overt censorship but through subtle mechanisms like ownership and funding, sourcing, flak, and common enemy narratives. Ownership and funding are when media outlets owned by large corporations or influenced by advertisers may avoid stories that harm corporate interests. Sourcing is the over-reliance on official sources and experts, often from powerful institutions, which limits the diversity of perspectives. Flak is a negative response from powerful actors to media criticism, which can deter future critical reporting. Consider anti-communism/anti-terrorism (or similar "common enemy" narratives) which use a widely accepted ideology to frame issues and delegitimize dissenting voices. Calling someone a terrorist, for example, elicits a powerful framing that hacks our cognitive vulnerabilities. These methods create a consensus that often serves the interests of power, making it difficult for the public to access truly independent perspectives.

This leads to a crisis of trust, which is a widespread erosion of faith in institutions, traditional media, and expert authority. Decades of perceived failures, broken promises, and exposure to misinformation have created fertile ground for manipulation. When people no longer trust established sources of information, they become more susceptible to alternative narratives, including those from malicious actors or extremist groups who promise "the real truth." This trust deficit is a critical cognitive vulnerability, as it dismantles one of the primary safeguards against false information.

What are the unique digital age issues used in political and ideological exploitation?

- **Micro-Targeting**

  Political campaigns use vast amounts of personal data (from social media, browsing history, and consumer habits) to craft highly specific, personalized messages designed to appeal to individual voters' fears, hopes, and biases. This allows for psychological manipulation on an unprecedented scale, tailoring messages to exploit specific cognitive vulnerabilities of individuals, rather than groups.

- **Hyper-Partisan Echo Chambers**

  As discussed, algorithms on social media push users towards content that confirms their existing views, creating highly insulated ideological bubbles. Within these bubbles, partisan rhetoric is amplified, dissent is absent, and the "other side" is increasingly dehumanized, fostering extreme polarization and making civil discourse almost impossible.

- **The Speed of Disinformation**

  Political disinformation can spread virally across digital platforms at scale before traditional fact-checking mechanisms can even begin to address it. This can shape public opinion before the truth can catch up.

The weaponization of identity in politics, amplified by digital technologies, creates a landscape where cognitive vulnerabilities are not just exploited, but can be done at scale with limited investment barriers. This leads to profound societal fragmentation and a challenging environment for informed democratic participation.

PART III
Mitigating Against Cognitive Exploitation and Building Resiliency

CHAPTER 11
Individual Strategies for Cognitive Resilience

"The best fighter is never angry."
- Lao Tzu

While the threats to our minds are pervasive, the good news is that we are not helpless. Building cognitive defenses begins with individual awareness and the cultivation of specific mental habits. This part of the book outlines actionable strategies for building resiliency against the exploitation of our cognitive vulnerabilities.

The Scientific Method - Humanity's Reliable Path to Knowledge

Throughout history, human beings have sought to understand the world around them. From myths and folklore to philosophy and religious doctrine, countless systems have claimed to provide knowledge about reality. While many of these approaches have shaped culture and morality, only one method has consistently produced reliable, self-correcting, and universally applicable knowledge: the scientific method. It is the only reliable method of knowledge we have discovered. It is not owned by a group of elitists; the scientific method is for everyone to use.

The scientific method is not a rigid formula, but a disciplined process of inquiry built on observation, hypothesis, experimentation, and falsification. What sets it apart is its insistence on evidence that can be tested, verified, and reproduced. Where tradition and authority depend on the trustworthiness of their sources, science requires that claims be tested through systematic doubt and verified with evidence. In this way, knowledge is not granted by decree but earned through repeated confrontation with reality.

Other ways of knowing, such as intuition, revelation, or common sense, can provide personal insights, but they are deeply vulnerable to cognitive biases and cultural distortions. Human beings are prone to seeing patterns where none exist, to confusing correlation with causation, and to clinging to beliefs that feel comforting rather than true. The scientific method works precisely because it recognizes these weaknesses and creates structures to counteract them. Peer review, replication, and the willingness to discard even long-held theories when evidence demands it are safeguards against the errors of individual judgment.

The fruits of this method are undeniable. Modern medicine, electricity, space exploration, computing, and our understanding of DNA are all products of science's self-correcting rigor. Where superstition once attributed disease to spirits or divine punishment, science identified pathogens and created vaccines that have saved millions of lives. Where speculation once limited humanity to Earth, science has carried us to the moon and beyond. Each advancement rests not on unquestioned authority but on the cumulative, tested insights of generations.

Critics sometimes argue that science is not the only valid way of knowing. They point to art, ethics, or spirituality. These domains can enrich the human experience, yet they do not yield knowledge about the external world in the same way science does.

In the end, the strength of the scientific method lies in its humility. It does not claim the final truth but the provisional truth, and it is always open to revision in light of new evidence. Far from being a weakness, this openness is its greatest power. It ensures that science is not dogma but an ongoing journey, one that continually refines humanity's understanding of reality.

For all of human history, people have sought certainty. The scientific method does not provide absolute certainty, but it does offer the most reliable, self-correcting, and universally valid way of distinguishing fact from fiction. In a world full of noise, bias, and misinformation, the scientific method remains humanity's greatest discovery, the only trustworthy method we have for turning curiosity into knowledge. In addition to the scientific method being fundamental to our resiliency, critical thinking helps give us a better understanding of information and evidence.

Critical Thinking

The foundation of any effective cognitive defense is critical thinking. This is not about being cynical, but about fostering healthy skepticism and a proactive, inquisitive approach to knowledge.

Critical thinking is a proactive and inquisitive approach to knowledge that goes beyond passive acceptance. It is the ability to analyze information objectively, evaluate evidence, and reason clearly to form sound judgments. Instead of accepting ideas at face value or relying on biases and assumptions, critical thinkers question, test, and refine their understanding. It's not just about what you think, but how you think. Critical thinking is the foundational skill for building cognitive defenses against exploitation.

At its core, critical thinking involves:

- **Clarity** -> <u>Asking</u>: What exactly does this mean?
- **Accuracy** -> <u>Checking</u>: Is this true? How do I know?
- **Logic** -> <u>Considering</u>: Do the reasons support the conclusion?
- **Fairness** -> <u>Asking</u>: Am I considering other perspectives?
- **Relevance** -> <u>Questioning</u>: Does this evidence matter to the issue?

The Cognitive Discipline of a Critical Thinker

To become a critical thinker, you must transform your cognitive habits from a passive, System 1 default to an active, System 2 discipline. This journey requires you to become your own mental security expert, systematically auditing your thought processes for vulnerabilities. The primary goal is to disarm your non-truth-seeking optimizers, such as the Ego, Tribal, and Belief optimizers, and allow the "discovery" or "truth" optimizers to take control.

This is a continuous act of self-correction, requiring you to actively choose intellectual honesty over emotional comfort. When you encounter a piece of information that triggers a strong emotional reaction, especially outrage or defensiveness, your non-truth-seeking optimizers are likely at work. The critical thinker's first move is to pause and ask a simple, yet profound, question: "Am I asking questions about a contradiction, or am I employing evasive tactics?" This moment of metacognition is where resilience is born.

How to Develop Critical Thinking Skills

Becoming a critical thinker is a lifelong practice. The following strategies will help you train your mind to think more critically and to navigate a world full of manipulation and misinformation.

- **Ask Better Questions:** Move beyond simple questions like "what happened?" and ask "why did it happen?", "what are the alternatives?", and "who benefits if I believe this?".
- **Recognize Cognitive Biases:** Learning about mental shortcuts like confirmation bias, anchoring, and groupthink is the first step toward mitigating their influence on your judgment.
- **Seek Evidence, Not Just Opinions:** Don't rely solely on authority or popularity. Actively look for credible sources, data, and sound reasoning behind any claim.

- **Practice Perspective-Taking:** Challenge yourself to argue from an opposing viewpoint. This exercise forces you to see the blind spots in your own reasoning and helps you better understand why others might interpret information differently.
- **Slow Down Your Thinking:** As Daniel Kahneman explains in *Thinking, Fast and Slow*, critical thinking requires you to deliberately engage your System 2 (the slow, analytical mind) rather than relying on the fast, intuitive System 1.
- **Be Comfortable with Uncertainty:** A good critical thinker can say, "I don't know yet" and resist the urge for a quick, neat answer. This patience is a powerful defense against manipulators who exploit your need for cognitive closure.
- **Reflect and Self-Correct:** After making a decision or forming a belief, revisit it later. Ask yourself, "What did I miss? What would change my mind?" This habit reinforces a growth mindset and keeps your mind agile.

Learning How the World Works

Learning how the world works is an important aspect of critical thinking. While critical thinking focuses on *how* you process information, learning how the world works is about building a mental model of reality that is as accurate and useful as possible. It's about understanding the underlying systems and forces that drive events, not just the events themselves. This helps to inform better questions required to think critically. Experts, for example, know what questions to ask about their domain, whereas a novice will often ask very poor questions that do not properly interrogate a claim or clarify information.

This involves developing an understanding of:

- **Systems** -> Seeing how economics, politics, and cultures interconnect rather than treating them as isolated pieces.

- **Incentives** -> Recognizing that people, organizations, and nations often act according to their self-interest, not just ideals.
- **Patterns** -> Noticing recurring dynamics in history and human behavior.
- **Cause and Effect** -> Looking beyond surface events to the structures and forces that drive them.

A Declining Bee Population

Imagine you're a city planner and you notice a significant decline in the local bee population. Without understanding how the world works your questions might be superficial and focused on immediate, visible problems.

You may ask:

- *"Why are there fewer bees?"*
- *"What do we need to do to get more bees back?"*
- *"Can we just buy more bees and release them?"*

These questions don't address the underlying causes. They focus on the symptoms (fewer bees) rather than the disease (the reasons for their decline).

With understanding how the world works you would have a basic knowledge of ecology, biology, and environmental science. This allows you to think more critically and ask targeted, insightful questions.

You may ask:

- *"What are the primary food sources for bees in this area, and have they been impacted by new landscaping or pesticide use?"* (This question considers the role of food and habitat.)
- *"Are there any new diseases or parasites affecting bee colonies, and how might they have been introduced?"* (This question considers biological threats.)

- *"Have there been changes in local agricultural practices or urban development that could be affecting the bees' migration patterns or nesting sites?" (This question considers human impact and habitat disruption.)*

By understanding the interconnectedness of ecosystems, you can ask questions that are relevant, address the underlying causes, and lead to more effective solutions. Instead of simply trying to replace the bees, you can work on creating a sustainable environment for them. This deeper understanding is what transforms a simple observation into a powerful critical inquiry.

How to Develop a Better Understanding of the World

- **Read Widely and Across Disciplines**

  The world is a complex puzzle, and subjects like history, economics, and psychology each provide a different piece. For example, learning about supply and demand helps explain markets, while evolutionary psychology helps explain tribalism and group conflict.

- **Study History Deeply**

  History often "rhymes." Patterns of wars, financial crises, and social movements repeat, offering a valuable perspective that is difficult to gain otherwise.

- **Follow Incentives, Not Just Narratives**

  When you see a decision or action, ask: "Who gains?" and "What is motivating this?". This helps you look beyond the public narrative to the underlying drivers.

- **Compare Models, Don't Marry Them**

  No single ideology—whether it's capitalism or socialism—explains everything. Challenge yourself to cross-check perspectives and integrate insights from multiple worldviews. Ideology does not resolve to the complexity of reality. An ideology is a set of rules and relationships that create a cognitive tool kit to understand a domain. An ideology is a blunt tool at best that gets co-opted into tribal identities, where they lose most of their meaning.

- **Think in Feedback Loops, Not Straight Lines**
  Most complex systems, from climate change to financial markets, operate in loops with delayed effects. Learn to look for the feedback, not just the immediate action (systems thinking).

Systems thinking is an approach to understanding how things influence one another within a whole entity by examining the interconnections, relationships, and interactions of a system's components rather than just isolated elements. It's a holistic and integrative way of seeing the "big picture" to understand complex issues, identify patterns, predict ripple effects, and develop more comprehensive, sustainable solutions, contrasting with traditional methods that focus on breaking systems down into individual parts. Systems thinking and learning all the domains (subjects) of the world are necessary for really understanding the world.

What are the subjects needed to understand the world? The list could be endless, but here is a baseline for what is needed:

- Life Science (e.g., Biology, Ecology, Environmental Science, Health, etc.)
- Physical Science (e.g., Physics, Geology, Astrophysics, Chemistry, etc.)
- Research Methods and Statistics
- Logic and Reasoning
- Philosophy of Knowledge (Epistemology)
- Philosophy of Ethics
- Psychology and Sociology
- Biopsychology (e.g., Cognitive Science, Neuroscience, Evolutionary Psychology, etc.)
- Humanities/Art/Linguistics
- Civics/Government
- Math (At least Algebra level)

- Technology (e.g., Computer Science, IT, Electrical Engineering, Data Science, etc.)
- Engineering (e.g., Civil Engineering, Architecture, how things are made, etc.)
- Language (Reading, Writing, and Comprehension)
- History
- Economics (Macro, Micro, Philosophy/Theory)
- Business/Finance
- Foreign Language

By committing to these intellectual disciplines, you can build a mind that is not merely reactive but truly resilient. It is a mind that can navigate the immense complexity of the modern world and is less susceptible to exploitation from both external manipulators and its own internal vulnerabilities. This approach requires a growth mindset, which is needed not just for critical thinking but also for a resilient mind in general.

How a Growth Mindset Helps Build Mental Resiliency

An important part of building cognitive resilience is adopting a growth mindset, a concept extensively popularized by psychologist Carol Dweck. This contrasts with a "fixed mindset." Someone with a fixed mindset believes their abilities, intelligence, and even personality traits are static and unchangeable. When faced with challenges or failures, they might interpret them as proof of their inherent limitations, leading to feelings of helplessness, avoidance of new experiences, and a reluctance to address their own cognitive biases.

Conversely, a growth mindset is the belief that one's abilities, intelligence, and personal qualities can be developed and improved through dedication and hard work. This perspective fundamentally shifts how an individual approaches information, challenges, and setbacks, making it a powerful tool for cognitive resilience.

Embracing Challenges and Learning from Failure

Instead of viewing difficulties or errors as evidence of inadequacy, a growth mindset sees them as opportunities for learning and growth. This directly counteracts the ego optimizers that can cause us to defend our flawed understanding or avoid uncomfortable truths. When you possess a growth mindset, the discomfort of being wrong or encountering contradictory information becomes an opportunity for potential improvement, rather than a threat to be avoided or rationalized away.

Overcoming the Dunning-Kruger Effect

The Dunning-Kruger Effect, as mentioned earlier, highlights how low information individuals often overestimate their competence, while high information individuals might underestimate theirs. A growth mindset encourages a more accurate self-assessment, as it fosters a genuine desire for improvement. Individuals are more likely to seek feedback, acknowledge gaps in their understanding, and remain open to learning from others, regardless of their perceived current skill level. This actively works against the "paradox of ignorance" where the less we know, the louder and more confidently we preach it.

Resisting Motivated Reasoning and Dogmatism

A fixed mindset can make individuals more prone to motivated reasoning, as they are invested in proving their existing beliefs are "right" to protect their fixed sense of self. A growth mindset, however, engages truth-seeking strategic optimizers. If intelligence and understanding are seen as fluid, there's less personal threat in updating beliefs based on new evidence. This makes individuals more adaptable and less likely to fall into the trap of rigid, unyielding worldviews that promote delusion.

Fostering Curiosity and Openness to Diverse Information

If learning is the goal, then new and even challenging information is welcomed rather than feared. This directly combats the insulating effects of echo chambers and confirmation bias. A growth mindset encourages active information seeking from varied sources, leading to a richer and more nuanced understanding of complex issues.

Building Emotional Regulation

The journey of learning and growth inevitably involves discomfort, frustration, and occasional failure. A growth mindset frames these emotions as part of the process, rather than as signals to give up. This emotional resilience enables individuals to manage things like fear that can trigger impulsive System 1 responses when faced with challenging information.

Integrating the growth mindset into our cognitive defense strategy means actively embracing the idea that our minds are not static fortresses but dynamic landscapes capable of continuous improvement and adaptation. This fundamental shift in perspective empowers us to see cognitive vulnerabilities not as inherent flaws, but as areas where we can consciously build strength, flexibility, and resilience.

Skepticism and Healthy Doubt

Rational skepticism means distinguishing between cynicism (a general distrust of everything) and constructive doubt (the willingness to question claims and assumptions, especially those that align too perfectly with your existing beliefs). As Carl Sagan famously advocated, extraordinary claims require extraordinary evidence. It means being open to being wrong and understanding that certainty is often a cognitive trap.

Approach to Knowledge

Prioritize "exploration and discovery" over "ego/belief protection." This requires an awareness to recognize when your ego, tribal, belief preservation, and other strategic optimizers are triggered. When you feel a strong emotional reaction to information, pause. Ask yourself: "Is my goal right now to find the truth, or to protect a pre-existing belief or my group's standing?" "Am I asking more questions about a contradiction or employing evasive tactics?" This self-awareness is the first step toward disarming motivated reasoning.

Evaluating Sources and Evidence (Lateral Reading)

In an age of abundant information, simply checking a source's "About Us" page is insufficient. Lateral reading, a technique advocated by Stanford University's civic online reasoning research, involves opening multiple tabs and researching the source itself while reading. Does Wikipedia say this source is biased? Do other reputable sources corroborate the claim? Who funds this organization? This moves beyond simply reading *what* a source says to investigating *who* is saying it and *why*.

Carl Sagan's Baloney Detection Kit

In *The Demon-Haunted World*, Sagan provides a practical toolkit for critical inquiry. This "Baloney Detection Kit" includes:

- Independent confirmation of the "facts."
- Encouraging substantive debate on the evidence.
- Do not be overly attached to a hypothesis just because it's yours.
- Quantifying where possible.
- Considering multiple working hypotheses.
- Not confusing correlation with causation.
- Asking whether the hypothesis can be disproven.
- Using Occam's Razor (choosing the simpler explanation).

- Being wary of appeals to authority.

Identifying Logical Fallacies

Becoming adept at recognizing flawed arguments is a powerful defense. Practice identifying logical fallacies not just in political speeches but in everyday contexts, like advertising. For example, recognizing an *ad hominem* attack allows you to dismiss the personal insult and refocus on the substance of the argument.

Understanding Cognitive Biases

Self-awareness of one's own susceptibility to biases is very useful. Knowing about confirmation bias, for instance, allows you to actively seek out diverse viewpoints rather than passively consuming only what confirms your existing beliefs. Acknowledge that you are human and therefore biased, and work to mitigate your own self-influence.

Metacognition (Thinking About Thinking)

Metacognition involves developing self-awareness of your own cognitive processes, strengths, and weaknesses. It means taking a step back from your thoughts and analyzing *how* you are thinking. "Why am I feeling this way about this information? What assumptions am I making? Am I being swayed by emotion or logic?" This self-reflection is a powerful tool for cognitive resilience.

Emotional Regulation

Strong emotions, as discussed, can hijack rational thought. Strategies for managing emotions are needed to avoid impulsive decisions and resist emotionally driven manipulation. Techniques like mindfulness, deep breathing, and taking a deliberate "pause" before reacting can create the necessary space for System 2 to engage. If you're feeling intensely angry or afraid, defer important judgments until you can calm your mind.

Information Diet

Just as we curate our food intake, we must curate our news and information inputs. Actively seek diverse and reputable perspectives. This means intentionally following sources from different political leanings, different countries, and different disciplines. Avoid relying on a single source or algorithmic feed for all your information. Consider limiting exposure to highly sensational or outrage-inducing content, which is designed to keep you engaged through emotional hooks.

Avoiding Both-Sides-ism (False Equivalency Fallacy)

Avoiding both-sides-sim means understanding that presenting two "sides" can create a false balance for issues with clear factual disparity. For example, giving equal airtime to a climate scientist and a climate change denier implies an equal weight of evidence that does not exist. Critical thinking requires evaluating claims based on the strength of evidence, not merely on the existence of opposing viewpoints.

The Power of Slow Thinking

In an age of instantaneity, deliberately engaging System 2 for complex decisions is a revolutionary act. When faced with significant information or a decision, resist the urge for an immediate reaction. Take time to research, reflect, and consult multiple perspectives. This "slow thinking" allows for more methodical, logical, and rational processing, reducing the likelihood of falling prey to System 1 biases and manipulative urgency.

Building Cognitive Empathy

Cognitive empathy involves understanding the motivations and reasons behind others' beliefs, even if you profoundly disagree with them. It is not about condoning harmful beliefs but about recognizing the underlying human needs (like security, belonging, or meaning) that might lead someone to adopt a particular worldview. This fosters better communication, reduces tribal conflict, and allows for more effective engagement across ideological divides.

Resisting Motivated Reasoning

Controlling our motivated reasoning is perhaps the most challenging, yet most important, individual strategy. It requires a fundamental commitment to the motivation of truth and discovery above all other personal or tribal motivations. When you find yourself strongly wanting a particular belief to be true, or strongly wanting an opposing belief to be false, recognize that your strategic optimizers are at work. Consciously choose to consider contradictory evidence with an open mind, even if it causes discomfort. Focus on the motivation of discovery over your transient enculturated identity or need to prove yourself as always right. Smart people will see someone as a learner who is more mature than someone who always has to be right. Be mindful of the strategic optimizer triggers that pull you into non-truth-seeking motivated reasoning. This continuous self-correction and growth is needed to build a resilient mind.

The Story of Marcus - A Case Study in Cognitive Resilience

Marcus, a 45-year-old software engineer, considered himself a rational person. He prided himself on his intelligence and data-driven approach to life. He wasn't a conspiracy theorist; he trusted science and experts. One day, a friend shared a series of posts on a new social media platform about a "miracle health supplement" that supposedly cured a range of chronic illnesses. The posts featured emotional testimonials and linked to a website filled with scientific-sounding jargon and charts.

Initially, Marcus's System 1 was intrigued. The testimonials were compelling, and the website's design was sleek and professional, triggering his trust bias. His "self-interest optimizer" was also engaged; he had a relative with a chronic condition, and the idea of a simple cure was emotionally appealing. A fixed mindset might have led him to dismiss the information outright if he considered himself above such things, or to accept it uncritically due to his emotional connection. But Marcus, having worked on his cognitive defenses, decided to engage his System 2.

Instead of sharing the post or buying the product, he began to think critically. He started by asking critical thinking questions:

- **Clarity** -> *"What exactly does this mean?"* He realized the claims were vague, using terms like "detoxifying" and "balancing energy" without clear definitions.
- **Accuracy** -> *"Is this true? How do I know?"* He opened a new tab to research the company and the supplement's key ingredients. Using the principle of lateral reading, he looked for information from medical journals and reputable health organizations, not just the company's own website. He found no independent clinical trials supporting the claims.
- **Logic** -> *"Do the reasons support the conclusion?"* The website claimed the supplement worked because it was "natural." Marcus recognized this as the appeal to nature fallacy. He reasoned that just because something is natural doesn't mean it's effective or safe.
- **Fairness** -> *"Am I considering other perspectives?"* He consciously sought out critiques of the product and found a consumer protection report detailing the company's deceptive marketing practices. He also considered his friend's perspective, realizing their belief likely stemmed from a genuine desire to help, not malicious intent.

- **Relevance** -> *"Does this evidence matter to the issue?"* He found a list of the supplement's ingredients, but without clinical data on their combined effect, the list was irrelevant to the claim of a "miracle cure."

As he continued to research, Marcus felt a flicker of defensiveness. His Ego Optimizer wanted to believe he had found a hidden truth. But he practiced metacognition, taking a step back to ask himself, "Am I trying to find the truth, or am I trying to be right?" He chose to prioritize intellectual honesty. He was also comfortable with uncertainty, accepting that he didn't have a definitive answer as to why the company was so deceptive, but he had enough evidence to conclude the product was a scam.

He then reflected on the experience. He realized the initial emotional appeal and his trust in his friend were his primary vulnerabilities. He shared his findings with his friend, not with a sense of superiority, but with cognitive empathy, explaining his process without shaming them. This experience reinforced his commitment to the growth mindset, solidifying his understanding that even a smart person must continuously train their mind against its own vulnerabilities.

CHAPTER 12
Digital World Safety Guide

"The measure of intelligence is the ability to change."
- Albert Einstein

Navigating the digital landscape requires more than just traditional cybersecurity. It demands an approach covered by the discipline called cyberpsychology. Cyberpsychology is the interdisciplinary study of the psychological effects of technology on human behavior and experience, examining how digital interactions, online identities, and the internet influence human cognition and social behavior. It explores topics such as online anonymity, the online disinhibition effect, digital addiction, impression management, social engineering in cybercrime, and the human factors in cybersecurity, providing crucial insights into our increasingly connected digital lives. This chapter provides practical advice for staying cognitively safe online, building on the vulnerabilities discussed earlier.

The Foundations of Resilience

In the ever-evolving landscape of digital threats, the traditional focus on technical security measures is no longer sufficient. The modern adversary targets the human mind, exploiting cognitive biases, emotional vulnerabilities, and social dynamics. It is important to build resilience, both psychological and technical, as a defense against online threats. Online resilience is not just about avoiding attacks; it's about developing psychological resilience to withstand and recover from them, transforming the human element from a point of weakness to a strength. Cyberpsychology offers a roadmap for cultivating resilience. Cyberpsychologists recognize that our online behaviors are driven by mental processes and emotional states that can be trained and strengthened. By understanding these mechanisms, we can move from a reactive posture to a proactive one, building a mindset that is inherently resistant to online cognitive attacks.

Proactive Cyberpsychology Guidelines

Beyond technical security, a proactive approach to online safety involves understanding and managing our psychological responses and behaviors. These strategies empower us to navigate the digital world with greater awareness and control. At the core of online resilience lies the ability to think critically and process information effectively. Cognitive strategies help us sharpen our mental tools, enabling us to navigate the digital world with greater awareness and control.

1. **Enhance Digital and Media Literacy**

    An important part of online resilience is the ability to critically evaluate and process digital content. Cyberpsychology research on cognitive biases in online information processing helps us understand how our brains are susceptible to manipulation. These insights enable individuals to develop the cognitive skills to recognize manipulation tactics and deception, such as phishing emails, fake news, and online scams. This isn't about becoming a cynic; it's about becoming an informed, discerning consumer of digital content.

2. **Cultivate Critical Thinking**

    The fast-paced nature of the internet often demands quick reactions. Instead of reacting to online triggers with fear or panic, critical thinking encourages a "pause and verify" mindset. This cognitive pause helps individuals question the credibility of information, verify identities, and avoid impulsive actions that could lead to security breaches or emotional distress. A 2018 study on online deception found that individuals who took a moment to mentally step back and analyze a request were significantly less likely to fall for social engineering attacks.

3. **Develop Self-Awareness**

    Our digital habits are often unconscious. By understanding your own mental processes and digital habits, you can recognize signs of online stress, compulsion, or addiction and take corrective action. Self-awareness allows for a healthier, more balanced approach to technology use, mitigating risks like burnout or excessive screen time. This includes understanding what kind of content triggers a negative emotional response and consciously choosing to avoid it.

Emotional Strategies for a Calm Response

Online attacks often prey on emotions, whether it's fear, anger, greed, or a need for validation. Emotional resilience is the capacity to manage and appropriately respond to these intense feelings, preventing them from becoming security vulnerabilities.

1. **Strengthening Emotional Regulation**

    The capacity to manage and appropriately respond to intense emotions is crucial for online resilience. Training in emotional regulation helps individuals stay calm and focused when faced with online negativity, harassment, or cyberbullying, rather than reacting impulsively. Studies on emotional intelligence show that individuals with strong emotional regulation skills are more likely to de-escalate online conflicts and less likely to engage in "flame wars."

2. **Practice Self-Compassion and Reframe Negative Narratives**

    Cyberpsychology-informed techniques help individuals avoid taking online harassment personally. By reframing negative comments or events, individuals can see them as reflections of the harasser's own issues rather than their own self-worth. This process, supported by research on cognitive reframing, shifts the internal narrative from "I am worthless" to "This person is acting out of their own issues."

3. **Leverage Positive Feedback Loops**
   Social media is often designed to trigger dopamine responses, leading to validation-seeking behavior. Cyberpsychology suggests consciously breaking these loops by focusing on self-worth that is not dependent on online metrics like likes or shares. This involves intentionally seeking out and engaging in activities that provide genuine, intrinsic rewards, thereby reducing the psychological dependence on external validation.

Behavioral and Social Strategies

Beyond the individual's inner world, resilience is built through concrete actions and strong social connections. These strategies translate psychological understanding into practical, everyday habits.

1. **Set and Enforce Boundaries**
   Establishing clear rules for digital engagement is key to maintaining digital well-being. Individuals can build resilience by limiting screen time, curating their social media feeds to filter out negativity, and utilizing privacy settings to control their online exposure. A 2019 study on digital well-being found a direct correlation between clear personal boundaries and a reduced sense of online stress and anxiety.

2. **Build a Strong Support Network**
   Strong online and offline support systems help individuals cope with difficult situations. Cyberpsychology research shows that having people to talk to, such as trusted friends, family, or online communities, can provide perspective and emotional backing during crises, acting as a buffer against the negative psychological effects of cyber attacks or harassment.

3. **Engage in "Upstanding" Behavior**

   Promoting positive online behavior and being willing to seek help are key to fostering supportive digital environments. Resilient individuals not only stand up for themselves but also support their peers when they are being targeted online. This collective action creates a more secure and psychologically safe online community for everyone.

4. **Train through Simulation**

   In a professional context, cyberpsychology-informed training can simulate cyber attacks and social engineering attempts. This allows individuals and teams to practice their response in a safe, controlled environment, building instinctive reactions and reducing human error. This type of training moves beyond simple awareness to muscle memory, making the correct response habitual.

Cybersecurity Safety

While psychological strategies form the foundation of resilience, they must be complemented by sound technical practices. This practical layer of defense ensures that our psychological fortitude is backed by a secure digital environment.

Protect Your Accounts

1. **Use Strong, Unique Passwords**

   These are your first line of defense against account takeovers. Create complex passwords for each account using a password manager to generate and store them securely.

2. **Enable Multi-Factor Authentication (MFA)**

   Add an extra layer of security by enabling 2-step verification for your accounts. Compromised accounts can be used by malicious actors to spread misinformation or manipulate your social circle, essentially turning you into an unwitting vector for their cognitive attack.

3. **Be Careful with Personal Information**

   Limit the amount of personal information you share online and avoid sharing sensitive details via email.

Secure Your Devices and Connections

1. **Keep Software Updated**

   Regularly update your operating systems, apps, and browsers to patch security vulnerabilities.

2. **Lock Your Devices**

   Use a PIN or password to lock your phone, tablet, and computer whenever you step away from them.

3. **Connect Securely**

   Avoid using public Wi-Fi for sensitive transactions; use a VPN or your phone's hotspot for a more secure connection.

4. **Secure Your Home Network**

   Change the default password for your home Wi-Fi router and use a strong password.

Practice Safe Online Habits

1. **Be Wary of Suspicious Links and Downloads**

   Do not click on suspicious links or download attachments from unknown sources. As highlighted in Chapter 1, phishing exploits urgency and authority biases. Always pause before clicking links or downloading attachments from unexpected sources. Verify the sender's identity through an independent channel (for example, call the company using a number from their official website, not from the email).

2. **Back Up Your Data**

   Regularly back up your important files to an external drive or cloud service to prevent data loss.

3. **Install Antivirus Software**

   Use reliable antivirus software to protect your devices from malware.

4. **Review Privacy Settings**

   Periodically check and adjust your privacy settings on social media and other online accounts.

5. **Use Secure Communication**

   Use encrypted messaging apps where possible. Understand that anything you post online can potentially be used out of context or for manipulation, contributing to your digital footprint and potential vulnerabilities.

Building Defenses Against Disinformation and Angertainment Media

The digital threat landscape evolves rapidly, requiring ongoing learning and adaptation to new online threats, new scams, and new forms of synthetic media. Building defenses against disinformation and angertainment media is especially important for cognitive resilience.

Be aware that sophisticated, often state-sponsored, disinformation campaigns exist to destabilize societies and influence elections. These campaigns leverage the viral mechanics of false information and target our cognitive biases. Look for signs of coordinated inauthentic behavior, or narratives that appear out of sync with reputable reporting.

Much of modern media, particularly cable news and social media influencers, has evolved to sell anger and outrage. By constantly highlighting conflicts, perceived injustices, and threats, they activate our fear and prejudice optimizers. This keeps us in a heightened emotional state that is ripe for manipulation. Learn to recognize when content is designed to make you angry rather than inform you. Protect yourself by diversifying your news sources, seeking out calm, analytical reporting, and consciously disengaging from content that provokes only outrage without offering genuine insight.

Actively seek out news and perspectives outside your usual algorithmic feed to break out of your bubble. Use tools like news aggregators that offer diverse sources or simply commit to reading reputable news organizations with different editorial stances. This intentional effort helps to counteract the insulating effect of filter bubbles.

Regularly step away from screens and social media. This reduces information overload and allows your more deliberate thinking to rest and recalibrate. Practicing mindful engagement, where you consciously reflect on why you are consuming certain content and how it makes you feel, can break addictive dopamine loops.

An Example of Cognitive Resilience in Action

Consider the story of Sarah, a diligent professional who prided herself on being well-informed. Like many people, she relied heavily on her social media feed for news and updates. One evening, a video clip appeared on her timeline. It was a short, dramatic segment with a headline claiming a local community council had secretly voted to defund a popular public service, all to benefit a wealthy developer. The post came from an account she didn't recognize, but it was being shared by dozens of her friends and acquaintances.

The video was professionally edited and filled with clips of angry citizens and a narrator with a furious, authoritative voice. The comments section was ablaze with outrage. Sarah felt her own anger rising. This was exactly the kind of injustice that frustrated her. Without a second thought, she hit the "share" button, adding a comment about how corrupt the local government was.

For the next few days, her social media algorithms adjusted based on her engagement. Her feed became a constant stream of similar stories: more perceived injustices, more conflicts, and more angertainment media designed to keep her in a state of righteous anger. Each post acted like a spark, feeding her outrage and keeping her emotionally charged. Her worldview began to narrow, seeing everything through the lens of a battle between "us" and "them." She was caught in a filter bubble of her own creation, unknowingly reinforcing her biases with every click.

Then, a friend, a person who always seemed to be level-headed, sent her a direct message. "Hey, I saw that post you shared. Did you happen to read the official city report on the vote?"

Reluctantly, Sarah decided to check. She went to the city council's official website and found the full minutes of the meeting. The report detailed a completely different story. The vote was not to defund a service but to reallocate a small portion of its budget for a specific, public-facing project. It was a mundane, complex topic with a balanced, less sensational outcome. The viral video she had shared was a carefully edited piece of disinformation, designed to create anger and division by distorting the truth.

The realization was a shock. Sarah felt a wave of embarrassment, but more importantly, she felt a profound sense of relief. She had been living in a heightened emotional state, and seeing the reality was like stepping out of a storm.

Over the next week, she decided to take a digital detox, a break from her usual social media habits. She put her phone away for hours at a time, allowing her mind to rest from the constant stream of triggers. During this time, she began to read news from a wider range of sources, including reputable news organizations with different editorial stances. She started to practice mindful engagement, asking herself, "Why am I looking at this? How does this content make me feel?"

Sarah learned to recognize when content was designed to make her angry rather than inform her. She trained herself to look for signs of coordinated inauthentic behavior, and she developed a healthy skepticism toward emotionally charged narratives. Her journey from reactive anger to proactive resilience transformed her online experience. She was no longer a puppet on the strings of disinformation and outrage but an informed, deliberate navigator of the digital world.

Your digital world has a direct impact on your mental health. Protecting yourself requires active, informed engagement and healthy skepticism towards the raw digital world. Online safety education is not a one-time lesson but a continuous process. By integrating these cognitive, emotional, behavioral, and technical strategies, you can build a holistic defense.

CHAPTER 13
Societal Solutions and Collective Resilience

"If we are to have peace on Earth, our loyalties must become ecumenical rather than tribal."
- Albert Einstein

While individual cognitive defense is essential, the scope of the cognitive attack surface extends far beyond the individual. Building genuine resilience against manipulation and delusion requires societal solutions and collective resilience. This involves ethical considerations for collective action and cooperation, especially in a world where forces often push people to differentiate.

Ethics of Societal Action

How can we ethically create and manage diversity and cooperation in a world prone to tribalism? This necessitates confronting motivations that lead people to differentiate and solidify "us vs. them" mentalities. We must revisit the paradox of tolerance in which unbounded tolerance for intolerance can lead to the destruction of tolerance itself. Solutions often involve defining clear boundaries for permissible discourse, especially when speech incites violence or undermines democratic processes.

In terms of ethics and tolerance, it's important to differentiate between various forms of identity. Biological identity is that which we are fundamentally and cannot change, such as sex, gender identity, or race. Ideological identity is our beliefs and political affiliations. Cultural identity is the culture we identify as being a part of. Religious identity is the religion we believe in and are a member of. Not all identities hold ethically equal weight in societal consideration. A biological identity, for example, is not something we can change; it is just who we are. We need to create an ethical framework that prioritizes human dignity and universal rights while acknowledging and respecting legitimate differences. This framework should guide how we navigate identity politics without descending into destructive tribalism.

The Paradox of Free Speech Absolutism & How Unbounded Expression Can Silence Voices

Free speech is often heralded as the cornerstone of a democratic society, which is a safeguard against tyranny, a catalyst for progress, and a tool for truth. Yet when taken to its extreme, free speech absolutism, which is the belief that all speech should be protected without exception, can paradoxically erode the very freedom it seeks to uphold. This contradiction reveals itself not in abstract theory, but in the lived experience of individuals navigating increasingly hostile public discourse.

At the heart of this paradox lies the amplification of harmful speech. Bad actors weaponize free speech to dominate the narrative and shut down dissent. In environments where all speech is permitted, including hate speech, harassment, and disinformation, marginalized voices often become collateral damage. The absence of boundaries allows dominant or aggressive actors to flood the space with rhetoric that intimidates, excludes, or overwhelms others. This is even more true now, where bad actors can leverage social media. Victims of abuse may self-censor or withdraw entirely, not because they lack ideas, but because the cost of speaking becomes too high. In this way, absolutism does not create a level playing field; instead, it tilts it toward those most willing to weaponize speech.

Legal absolutism further complicates the landscape by dismantling the delicate balance between competing rights. Traditional free speech jurisprudence weighs expression against other societal values, such as equality, safety, and dignity. Absolutist frameworks discard this nuance, elevating speech above all else, even when it incites violence or discrimination. Recent legal decisions have demonstrated how this hierarchy can undermine civil rights protections, allowing speech-based exemptions to anti-discrimination laws. Over time, this erodes the pluralistic foundation that makes free speech viable in the first place.

The collapse of moderation mechanisms on digital platforms offers another cautionary tale. Content moderation is not censorship; it is rather a form of stewardship. It ensures that discourse remains inclusive, constructive, and safe. Yet under absolutist logic, moderation is often vilified, leading to environments where misinformation, trolling, and abuse flourish unchecked. The result is not more speech, but less meaningful speech. The signal-to-noise ratio deteriorates, and public discourse devolves into a cacophony where truth and civility are drowned out.

This cognitive overload has deep implications. When everything is allowed, the human mind struggles to discern truth from falsehood. The marketplace of ideas becomes polluted, not by diversity of thought, but by deliberate manipulation. In such conditions, free speech loses its epistemic value, and it no longer serves as a conduit for understanding but as a tool for distortion.

Ultimately, free speech thrives not in a vacuum, but in a carefully cultivated ecosystem. Absolutism bulldozes that ecosystem, often empowering the powerful while silencing the vulnerable. It is a classic example of how freedom without responsibility can become oppression in disguise. To preserve the integrity of free expression, we must embrace a more nuanced approach that recognizes the interplay between rights, responsibilities, and the social conditions that make speech truly free.

Education as a Shield Against Weaponized Speech and Disinformation

In our digital world, where information travels instantly and narratives can be manipulated with precision, societies face unprecedented risks from weaponized speech and disinformation. These tools aim to destabilize communities, erode trust in institutions, and exploit social divisions. One of the most effective defenses against such threats lies not in censorship or surveillance, but in education.

Education equips individuals with the critical thinking skills needed to evaluate claims, weigh evidence, and recognize manipulative tactics. A well-educated public is less likely to accept sensational claims at face value and more inclined to cross-check information against credible sources. This capacity for skepticism fosters resilience, reducing the impact of falsehoods designed to inflame fear or anger.

Beyond critical analysis, education strengthens social cohesion. When people understand history, civics, and the diverse perspectives within their own society, they become less vulnerable to polarizing narratives that paint "us versus them." In this way, education not only trains individuals to spot lies but also fosters empathy and tolerance, weakening the divisive power of disinformation campaigns.

Education promotes media literacy, which includes the ability to navigate digital environments thoughtfully. By teaching students how algorithms shape what they see online and how rhetorical strategies are used to sway emotions, societies create citizens who can engage with information responsibly.

Education is a long-term investment in national resilience. By cultivating critical minds and empathetic communities, it creates a public that is far less susceptible to manipulation, safeguarding democracy against the corrosive effects of weaponized speech and disinformation.

Education Reform is perhaps the most foundational societal solution. Advocating for curricula that build resiliency from early ages is important.

What should we teach children and adolescents for societal resilience?

- **Critical Thinking Skills**: How to analyze arguments, identify logical fallacies, and evaluate evidence rigorously.
- **Media Literacy**: How to deconstruct media messages, recognize bias, distinguish between fact and opinion, and understand the economic and political forces shaping information.
- **Digital Citizenship**: Responsible and ethical behavior online, understanding the impact of their digital footprint, and recognizing online manipulation tactics.
- **Emotional Intelligence**: How to understand and manage their own emotions and empathize with others, which helps to mitigate the emotional hijacking that fuels many cognitive attacks.
- **Self-Regulation**: Teach children to manage their emotions and impulses through techniques like mindfulness or healthy coping strategies.
- **Optimism & Hope**: Help them cultivate a positive outlook, focus on past successes, and believe in a better future.
- **Purpose & Meaning**: Encourage them to find a sense of purpose and meaning in their lives, which can be a powerful motivator for adapting to adversity.
- **Empower Through Helping**: Engage children in helping others through age-appropriate volunteer work or assisting with tasks, which can build their sense of agency.
- **Diversity**: Teach children about other cultures and show them our shared humanity.

By embedding these skills from kindergarten through higher education, we can raise a generation with more robust cognitive defenses.

Applying the cybersecurity concept of "Information Assurance" to cognitive security provides a valuable framework. Information Assurance (Cognitive Security Framework) aims to ensure the integrity, availability, and confidentiality of information systems.

For cognitive security, we can adapt these principles:

- **Confidentiality**
  Ensuring information is shared only with the intended audience and context. In a cognitive sense, this means respecting the privacy of thought and avoiding coercive sharing of beliefs, as well as being aware of how personal data is harvested for manipulative micro-targeting.
- **Integrity**
  Ensuring the intended message is shared without manipulation or distortion. This means supporting truthful reporting, fact-checking, and combating deepfakes, so that the information people receive is uncorrupted.
- **Availability**
  Ensuring access to accurate and necessary information when needed. This means combating censorship, promoting open access to diverse sources, and ensuring that reliable information is easily discoverable amidst noise and falsehoods.

Technological interventions offer another layer of societal resilience by designing our digital systems to be less susceptible to cognitive exploitation.

- **Algorithmic Transparency and Accountability**
  Holding platforms responsible for the societal impact of their algorithms. This involves understanding how algorithms promote content, identifying and mitigating biases, and ensuring that platforms do not inadvertently amplify harmful or polarizing narratives.

- **Fact-Checking Initiatives and Labeling**

    Support independent verification efforts and implement clear, prominent labeling of false or misleading content on social media and news platforms. This empowers users to make more informed judgments about the veracity of information.

- **Designing Platforms for Healthy Discourse**

    Encouraging platform design that promotes constructive engagement, civil debate, and discourages harmful interactions like harassment, hate speech, and the spread of disinformation. This might involve features that encourage thoughtful responses, diverse viewpoints, and consequences for malicious behavior.

- **AI in Identifying and Mitigating Malicious Cognitive Attacks**

    The potential of artificial intelligence to detect and counter sophisticated disinformation campaigns and manipulation attempts is immense. AI can be used to identify coordinated inauthentic behavior, detect synthetic media, and flag potentially misleading content at scale. However, this must be developed and deployed ethically to avoid censorship or bias.

Finally, policy and regulation are needed to shape the information environment and increase societal resilience. This is a complex area, often balancing freedom of speech with the need to protect public discourse.

- **Combating Disinformation** - Legislative and regulatory efforts are needed to address disinformation, particularly concerning election integrity and public health messaging. This involves navigating the delicate balance with free speech dilemmas.

    Some Example Solutions
    - **Bad actor-focused solutions:** Targeting the creators and disseminators of disinformation, rather than the content itself, which helps address free speech concerns.

- **Social media identifying and authenticating users:** Stopping anonymous posting could reduce the spread of malicious content by making actors accountable.
- **Stopping platforms from allowing bad actors to leverage their systems for scale:** Regulations could hold platforms accountable for the amplification of harmful content by malicious entities.
- **Education for the population:** As seen in countries like Finland, robust public education campaigns on media literacy and critical thinking have proven highly effective in building societal resilience to disinformation.
- **Robust public broadcast systems:** Investing in well-funded, independent public media that prioritize factual reporting can provide a trustworthy source of information for the populace.

- **Protecting Data Privacy and Preventing Micro-Targeting** - Regulations like GDPR and CCPA aim to limit the exploitation of personal data for manipulative targeting. Stronger privacy laws can reduce the ability of political campaigns and marketers to create highly tailored psychological attacks.
- **Addressing the Harms of Social Media** - Policies to mitigate negative impacts on mental health, addiction, and social cohesion, perhaps through age restrictions, content moderation guidelines, or mandating design changes that reduce addictive features.
- **Ethical Guidelines for AI and Persuasive Technologies** - Developing ethical frameworks and regulations for the development and deployment of AI and technologies designed to influence human behavior. As AI becomes more sophisticated in its ability to generate persuasive content, clear ethical boundaries are essential to prevent misuse.

Beyond policies, fostering healthy discourse is paramount. This means actively promoting empathy, civil debate, and strategies for bridge-building across ideological divides. Encouraging active listening, respectful disagreement, and seeking common ground can counteract the polarizing effects of tribalism.

Finally, investing in mental health is an important, often overlooked, component of cognitive defense. Addressing underlying psychological vulnerabilities that make individuals more susceptible to exploitation and manipulation (such as anxiety, depression, loneliness, or a lack of purpose) makes them less prone to seeking solace or identity in extreme narratives. A mentally resilient population is inherently more resistant to cognitive attacks.

CHAPTER 14

Ambassadors of Enlightenment 2.0

*"The only thing necessary for the triumph of evil
is for good men to do nothing."*
- Edmund Burke

The Future of the Human Mind

In the pages of this book, we have navigated the intricate landscape of the human mind, identified our ancestral-based vulnerabilities, and learned how they are systematically exploited in our modern, hyper-connected world. We have seen that our brains, magnificent relics of evolutionary success, are simultaneously our greatest strength and our most significant weakness.

We began by defining the "cognitive attack surface," recognizing that our inherent cognitive biases, dual processing systems, and evolutionary predispositions make us ripe for manipulation. We explored how the brain's innate drive to tell stories, form worldviews, and seek tribal belonging can solidify beliefs into unyielding delusions, often through the mechanisms of cognitive dissonance and motivated reasoning. We then examined the insidious spread of "mind viruses" and social contagion, amplified exponentially by digital platforms. Finally, we saw how these vulnerabilities are deliberately exploited by malicious actors, from scam artists to cult leaders, and weaponized by politicians in the ongoing information war.

The Ongoing and Changing Battle

It is important to understand that cognitive attacks will not cease, and they will continuously evolve. Just as cybersecurity professionals constantly adapt to new threats, we must remain vigilant, adaptable, and innovative in our cognitive defenses. New technologies, new social dynamics, and new forms of exploitation will emerge, requiring a continuous commitment to understanding and counteracting them. This is not a battle to be won once and for all, but an ongoing strategic engagement.

Self-Awareness

Ultimately, the foundational first step toward a more robust individual and collective future lies in understanding one's own mind. Self-awareness of our biases, our emotional triggers, our default cognitive settings, and our susceptibility to influence is the most powerful shield we possess. Without this introspection, all external defenses are insufficient. Only by truly knowing how our own minds work can we begin to consciously override their ancient, often maladaptive, programming.

A Call to Action!

Awareness, however, is not enough. We need to take decisive action as individuals and as a society. This book is more than a guide; it is a call to arms. It is an invitation to you, the reader, to become an active participant in building a more resilient world.

This means:

- **Empowering Individuals:** By cultivating critical thinking, managing our emotional responses, and actively curating our information diets.
- **Empowering Educators:** By advocating for comprehensive curricula that teach cognitive defense from an early age.

- **Empowering Policymakers:** By supporting regulations that promote ethical technology design, combat disinformation, and protect mental well-being without stifling free expression.
- **Empowering Technologists:** By developing AI and digital platforms with ethical guidelines that prioritize human cognitive health and truth over mere engagement.

The future of human thought, reason, and social cohesion depends on our collective ability to understand, defend, and ultimately transcend our cognitive vulnerabilities. Let us rise to this challenge and create a new enlightenment revolution.

Recommended Reading:

- *The Scout Mindset* by Julia Galef
- *The Cyber Effect* by Mary Aiken
- *The Demon-Haunted World* by Carl Sagan
- *Evolutionary Psychology* by David M. Buss
- *The Blank Slate* by Steven Pinker
- *Why We Believe in God(s)* by J. Anderson Thomson
- *The Art of Invisibility* by Kevin Mitnick
- *Critical Thinking* by Tom Chatfield
- *Thinking, Fast and Slow* by Daniel Kahneman

www.ingramcontent.com/pod-product-compliance
Lightning Source LLC
Chambersburg PA
CBHW070629030426
42337CB00020B/3965